T0360634

Gossip, Organization and Work

The premise of this book is that research into gossip, organization, and work is an important idea whose time has come. A key feature of the book is the inclusion of 'practice points' showing how – and where – theory and/or research intersect with practice and vice versa. They are intended as signposts to future thinking and theorizing, tempting readers to venture outside of their 'home' disciplines and territories, conceptual comfort zones, and methodological mindsets. The overall aim of the book is to: (i) provide enough information for readers to decide where they might want to go next; (ii) offer some theoretical directions and ethical principles; and (iii) make suggestions regarding what academic-practitioner tools and techniques will help them along the way, including arts-based and mixed-methods research that focuses on real-world lived experience(s) of gossip.

It will be relevant to researchers at all stages of their career: from students at the start of their academic journey, to 'seasoned' scholars with more extensive experience. The book is also intended to be readable and relevant to practitioners with academic interests, who seek to reflect critically upon, and develop, their practice in times of turbulence and change and in the COVID-19 era.

Kathryn Waddington is reader in work and organisational psychology at the University of Westminster, UK.

State of the Art in Business Research
Series Editor: Geoffrey Wood

Recent advances in theory, methods and applied knowledge (alongside structural changes in the global economic ecosystem) have presented researchers with challenges in seeking to stay abreast of their fields and navigate new scholarly terrains.

State of the Art in Business Research presents shortform books which provide an expert map to guide readers through new and rapidly evolving areas of research. Each title will provide an overview of the area, a guide to the key literature and theories and time-saving summaries of how theory interacts with practice.

As a collection, these books provide a library of theoretical and conceptual insights, and exposure to novel research tools and applied knowledge, that aid and facilitate in defining the state of the art, as a foundation stone for a new generation of research.

Managing Decline
A Research Overview
Antti Sihvonen, Juha-Antti Lamberg and Henrikki Tikkanen

Gossip, Organization and Work
A Research Overview
Kathryn Waddington

Remote Working
A Research Overview
Alan Felstead

For more information about this series, please visit: www.routledge.com/State-of-the-Art-in-Business-Research/book-series/START

Gossip, Organization and Work

A Research Overview

Kathryn Waddington

Routledge
Taylor & Francis Group

LONDON AND NEW YORK

First published 2022
by Routledge
4 Park Square, Milton Park, Abingdon, Oxon OX14 4RN

and by Routledge
605 Third Avenue, New York, NY 10158

Routledge is an imprint of the Taylor & Francis Group, an informa business

© 2022 Kathryn Waddington

The right of Kathryn Waddington to be identified as author of this work has been asserted in accordance with sections 77 and 78 of the Copyright, Designs and Patents Act 1988.

All rights reserved. No part of this book may be reprinted or reproduced or utilised in any form or by any electronic, mechanical, or other means, now known or hereafter invented, including photocopying and recording, or in any information storage or retrieval system, without permission in writing from the publishers.

Trademark notice: Product or corporate names may be trademarks or registered trademarks, and are used only for identification and explanation without intent to infringe.

British Library Cataloguing-in-Publication Data
A catalogue record for this book is available from the British Library

Library of Congress Cataloging-in-Publication Data
Names: Waddington, Kathryn, author.
Title: Gossip, organization and work: a research overview/Kathryn Waddington.
Description: Abingdon, Oxon; New York, NY: Routledge, 2022. |
Series: State of the art in business research |
Includes bibliographical references and index.
Identifiers: LCCN 2021046373 (print) | LCCN 2021046374 (ebook) |
ISBN 9780367653002 (hardback) | ISBN 9780367653026 (paperback) |
ISBN 9780367652982 (ebook)
Subjects: LCSH: Communication in organizations. | Gossip. |
Corporate culture. | Organizational behavior.
Classification: LCC HD30.3 .W333 2022 (print) | LCC HD30.3 (ebook) |
DDC 650.01/4–dc23
LC record available at https://lccn.loc.gov/2021046373
LC ebook record available at https://lccn.loc.gov/2021046374

ISBN: 978-0-367-65300-2 (hbk)
ISBN: 978-0-367-65302-6 (pbk)
ISBN: 978-0-367-65298-2 (ebk)

DOI: 10.4324/9780367652982

Typeset in Times New Roman
by Deanta Global Publishing Services, Chennai, India

Dedicated to the fond memory of my parents
Nancy and Reg Croft

Contents

Illustrations

Figures

Tables

Boxes

Foreword

For the past 30 years, an impressive literature has developed on the communicative constitution of organization (CCO), resulting in some remarkable empirical and theoretical insights. As it is often the case with innovative research agendas, the starting point of this research programme was relatively simple: what if we could conceive of communication as not only happening *in* organizations but also constituting them? In other words, couldn't it be the case that *organization also happens in communication* (Taylor, 1988; Taylor and Van Every, 2000, 2011, 2014)? While communication used to be often treated as an afterthought or a variable among many others, CCO scholars have convincingly shown that communications should, in fact, be considered the building blocks of the organization (Cooren, 2000). As pointed out by Chester Barnard (1938) and later Karl Weick (1979), without communication, no organizing can indeed take place and no organization can be constituted.

In her insightful book, Kathryn Waddington invites us to explore new CCO territories by examining the constitutive dimension of gossip. If communication was previously relegated to an afterthought in organization studies, one could claim that gossip has also played this unfortunate role in CCO studies, possibly because of its negative connotation, as well as its elusive and slippery nature. Waddington shows, however, that this form of communication deserves our attention, especially as a pathway to organizational knowledge. While gossip is often depicted in pejorative terms, she convincingly shows that it could also be conceived as a reaction against social isolation and perceived injustice. In other words, members who gossip certainly tend to talk badly about a third person or about specific organizational events or processes, but this kind of talk can also, in some cases, be seen as constructive to the extent that it helps people make sense of situations that could worsen if nothing is done to correct them.

In other words, the complicit character of gossip should, according to Waddington, be reinterpreted as a way to not only collectively make sense of a situation but also constitute it in terms that deserve our attention. As she reminds us, gossip can allow members to detect errors, reveal safety issues, and expose unethical behaviours such as harassment and bullying. More than ever, gossip can therefore be reconceived as the first step towards the denunciation of problematic situations that too often plague our organizational world. In a time when speaking up is being more and more encouraged, gossiping might constitute the obligatory passage point by which people test their take on a situation to ultimately build a collective voice capable of raising their concerns.

Kathryn Waddington thus invites us to rehabilitate gossip, not because this form of communication would be always positive, but because it might constitute the *power of the weak*, that is, what Michel de Certeau (1984) calls the *tactic* by which members, who are subjected to specific environments, attempt to resist what they perceive to be forms of injustice. Gossip, according to this reinterpretation, could therefore be conceived as a weak form of constitution, but a form that might ultimately make a difference if people manage to make themselves heard.

François Cooren
University of Montreal

References

Barnard, C. I. (1938). *The functions of the executive.* Cambridge, MA: Harvard University Press.

Cooren, F. (2000). *The organizing property of communication.* Amsterdam/Philadelphia: John Benjamins.

De Certeau, M. (1984). *The practice of everyday life.* Berkeley, CA: University of California Press.

Taylor, J. R. (1988). *Une organisation n'est qu'un tissu de communications.* Montréal: Cahiers de recherches en communication.

Taylor, J. R., & Van Every, E. J. (2000). *The emergent organization. Communication as site and surface.* Mahwah, NJ: Lawrence Erlbaum Associates.

Taylor, J. R., & Van Every, E. J. (2011). *The situated organization: Case studies in the pragmatics of communication.* New York: Routledge.

Taylor, J. R., & Van Every, E. J. (2014). *When organization fails: Why authority matters.* New York: Routledge.

Weick, K. E. (1979). *The social psychology of organizing.* New York: Random House.

Preface

The origin of the book was my doctoral research in psychology in the late 1990s/early 2000s, when there was little substantive organizational literature and research into gossip. Clive Fletcher was a wise and skilled supervisor who encouraged me to venture into what at the time was very uncharted territory.

Acknowledgements

There are a number of people I would like to thank for their contributions to this book. Grant Michelson and Ad van Iterson, my 'comrades in gossip research and scholarship', continue to be my travelling companions. Content has also benefitted from conversations and comments on earlier drafts of chapters from Angela Carter, Julie Davies, Dean Fathers, Henrietta Hughes, Deborah Husbands and Nick O'Connor. Philippa Sully cast her critical eye over my writing and, along with Hannele Weir, provided stimulating conversations about art, music, literature, and life. Hannah Waddington helped with illustrations; Pamela and Geoff Sawyer and Ian Croft gave family support and gentle reminders to get out into the garden more.

1 Introduction

Gossip, organization, and work

Gossip, organization, and work: a travel guide

This chapter takes as its premise that the study of gossip, organization, and work in the 21st century represents an important idea whose time has come. It includes a brief history of gossip as a background to the chapters that follow, which provide directions for future research in the field. In keeping with the brief for this series, the book should be read as a 'travel guide' through a new and rapidly evolving area of business and organizational research. Readers and researchers will need to travel light in order to travel far in this new and rapidly evolving field; or to use Weick's (1996, p. 311) allegory, to 'drop their heavy tools', which means:

> Focus on relationships, use abstract concepts, bridge observations and abstractions, and articulate the values that matter. ... To remind ourselves of that is to restore lightness.

I hope the book will be relevant to researchers at all stages of their career: from doctoral researchers at the start of their academic journey, to 'seasoned' scholars with more extensive experience. I also hope the book is readable and accessible to practitioners with academic interests, and who seek to reflect critically upon and develop their practice in times of turbulence and change. The overall aim of the book is to: (i) provide enough information for readers to decide where they might want to go next; (ii) offer some theoretical directions and ethical principles; and (iii) make suggestions regarding what academic-practitioner tools and techniques will help them along the way, including arts-based and mixed-methods research. A key feature of the book is the inclusion of 'practice points', which aim to provide readers with insights into how theory and/or research interact with practice.

DOI: 10.4324/9780367652982-1

Gossip: an idea whose time has come

In 1852 the French novelist, poet, and dramatist Victor Hugo (1802–1885), in his essay 'Histoire d'un Crime' (translated as 'The history of a crime'), legendarily said: an invasion of armies can be resisted, but not an idea whose time has come (Robb, 1997). For business and organizational scholars, gossip is an important idea whose time has come, as this book hopes to illustrate. While gossip has featured in history, literature, and art (e.g., Fletcher, 2009; Martin, 2014; Tebbutt, 1995), it has – until relatively recently – been absent in organizational, management, and business research literature. This is both puzzling and 'disappointing that organizational scholars have generally failed to acknowledge and engage with gossip' (Oswick, in Waddington, 2012, p. xv). What is even more difficult to explain is why cognate areas such as organizational discourse, narrative, and communication studies have overlooked the phenomenon of gossip. Paradoxically, I suggest that COVID-19 has unexpectedly shed light onto gossip as an idea whose time has come, and which cannot now be ignored or overlooked.

COVID-19: bringing gossip into the foreground?

In 2020 and 2021, the coronavirus pandemic and associated lockdowns fundamentally altered the ways that people engage with work, and with each other. The term 'Zoom fatigue' – excessive amounts of close-up eye gaze, cognitive load, increased self-evaluation from staring at oneself on a screen, and constraints on physical mobility – has entered day-to-day conversations and research agendas (Bailenson, 2021). Overnight, the opportunities for casual conversations constituted as gossip before, during, and after face-to-face meetings (e.g., Hallett et al., 2009) disappeared, and with them the largely unrecognized benefits and consequences of gossip, such as the establishment of social bonds, strengthening of relationships, and as a means to promote cooperation (Dores Cruz et al., 2021). The functional role of gossip as a means of emotional expression and regulation (Martinescu et al., 2019; Waddington & Fletcher, 2005) has now been shown in sharp relief. COVID-19 has unexpectedly 'shone a light' on gossip. To paraphrase Joni Mitchell's lyrics from Big Yellow Taxi: you don't know what you've got (gossip as an organizational phenomenon worthy of serious scholarship) 'til it's gone. An unforeseen, and ironic, outcome of the pandemic, therefore, has been to bring gossip into the foreground – as a phenomenon worthy of research in hitherto overlooked fields of organizational discourse, narrative, and communication studies. Another reason why gossip is now coming steadily into the foreground is the emerging literature surrounding gossip as an early warning of organizational failure, which is considered next.

Gossip as an early warning of organizational failure

Recognition of the links between risk and reputation, and the 'sentinel function' of gossip as an early warning indicator of failure in healthcare and other organizations, systems, and teams, is beginning to grow (Kewell, 2007; Waddington, 2016, 2020):

> The sentinel function of gossip and rumour can be an early warning of serious issues within an organisation, including matters of patient welfare and safety. Clinicians in leadership and executive positions need to know how to manage gossip and rumour situations. (O'Connor et al., 2018, p. 32)

In healthcare, government-led inquiries/investigations illustrate the stark human, financial, and reputational costs of organizational failures. They also reveal that information about the antecedents of failure and scandal are often 'common knowledge' contained in gossip. For example, the UK *Kerr/ Haslam Inquiry* (HM Government, 2005) into two decades of sexual abuse of female psychiatric patients asked:

- How could it happen that abuse of patients, evidenced by the convictions of William Kerr and Michael Haslam, went undetected for so long?
- How could it be that the voices of the patients and former patients of William Kerr and Michael Haslam were not heard?
- Why were so many opportunities to respond and investigate missed?

The inquiry revealed a widespread belief within the local medical community, circulating as gossip and rumour, that something was extremely wrong with the practices of the two consultant psychiatrists. One of the inquiry's many recommendations was:

> In answer to the question – when should rumour etcetera—be acted upon, and in what form should that action be taken – *we can only invite further research.*
> (HM Government, 2005, p. 683, emphasis added)

There is clearly still much further research yet to be done; the above recommendation, as is so often the case with public inquiries, was neither funded nor implemented (Norris & Shepheard, 2017; Waddington, 2016).

Van Iterson and Clegg (2008) used the *Cole Inquiry* (2006) into the United Nations (UN) Oil-for-Food Programme as a case analysis of gossip, rumour, power, and politics. Their article makes an important research contribution in that it provides an organizational-level analysis of how gossip that spreads facts-based rumours can be understood in terms of their shifting role in circuits of power. A British diplomat with the UN identified that in 1999 she first heard gossip circulating in the UN that the Australian Wheat Board was in breach of the programme. In 2005 the UN Independent Inquiry Committee verified the information circulating as gossip and rumour. Van Iterson and Clegg (2008, pp. 1133–1134) concluded:

> However much an organization may assume that it has stabilized the circuits of power flowing through a specific arena, that arena is always capable of being reconfigured by other circuits, other actors – and gossip plays a key role in these relations.

These illustrative inquiries illustrate two key points: firstly, the relationship, and *difference*, between gossip and rumour, terms which are often used interchangeably in lay conversations. McAndrew (2019, p. 174) makes the critical point that researchers need to be more precise about the differences and distinguishing features, pointing out that rumours are unsubstantiated bits of information that may involve future events, people, or some other topic of collective interest; 'gossip is defined more specifically as talk about people'. However, Adkins (2017, p. 9, emphasis added), reflecting upon research into gossip episodes and narratives, argues that gossip is much more than just talk 'about people':

> It's clear that much of what conversationalists have self-identified as gossip isn't simply or merely personal in nature. In other words when we gossip, we aren't always just talking about people (let alone the behind their back part). To be specific … people gossip at work, a lot, and often what they're talking about (evaluatively, confidentially, sometime angrily) are *corporate or institutional events and actions*.

Therefore, the second key point is that government-led inquiries/investigations – which relate to organizational events and in/actions – provide a rich source of gossip-related empirical materials at group/community and organizational levels, available in the public domain for further analysis. Further research could potentially pre-empt inquiries into organizational failure and scandals and associated economic costs. Since 1990, UK central and devolved governments have spent at least £638.9 million on public inquiries, and this figure is rising (Norris & Shepheard, 2017). More importantly, further research could potentially prevent the terrible human costs of such failures and scandals. It would, however, be naïve to claim that this short book will be able to address fully the latter points, and future research into the sentinel function of gossip is certainly not an easy option. The complex ethical issues related to researching gossip are addressed in more detail in Chapter 4: 'Researching organizational gossip: ethical considerations'. Chapter 5: 'Future directions and pathways to practice-based knowledge' outlines methods and models of academic-practitioner inquiry, arising from recent research, and recommendations into creating 'speak-up' organizational cultures (Reitz & Higgins, 2019), which are now becoming part of the wider changing landscape of work.

The changing landscape of work

Dewe and Cooper (2021), in the *Work and Stress* title in this series, signalled that the future requires a change in thinking away from old and outdated models of 'jobs' and 'employees', which are 'increasingly irrelevant and obstruct innovation, growth and opportunity' (p. 179). How work gets done has changed fundamentally in recent decades. An increasing number of people now work independently, outside of organizations, in what has become known as the 'gig economy' – new business models produced by digital platforms. This has resulted in growing numbers of platform-enabled peer-to-peer businesses such as Airbnb and Uber (Spreitzer et al., 2017). The coronavirus pandemic – in addition to bringing the significance of gossip into the foreground – is also impacting globally upon society, business, and the economy (Meyer et al., 2021). This is radically changing the idea of work and how and where it happens. The full extent of the outcomes and impact of the pandemic remains to be written, but there will undoubtedly be consequences for what constitutes organization, organizations, and organizing. This raises critical issues regarding:

- The relevance and value of pre-pandemic research in the changing landscape of work.
- A need for new approaches and paradigms to guide future research in the field.

These issues will inevitably impact questions relating to *where, with whom, why, and how does gossip occur in contemporary work environments and organizations*. To remain relevant, research into gossip must adapt to this new world of work. I contend that rather than relying solely on 'traditional, tried and tested' maps, methodologies, and methods, new ways of thinking are needed, framed by the orienting positions of:

- Gossip *and* organizations (Waddington, 2012).
- Qualitative methods in business and management research (Cassell et al., 2018).

Gossip and organizations

It is important to think about gossip *and* organizations, rather than gossip *in* organizations. This moves beyond simplistic notions of communication as the transmission of information and avoids the 'organization-as-container' metaphor, which in the field of communication studies is seen as outdated and problematic (Grant & Nyberg, 2011). Rejecting the idea of organizations as containers focuses future research towards the theoretical endeavour of the communicative constitution of organizations (CCO). CCO thinking and theorizing promotes the argument that discourse creates organizations; that organizations are invoked and maintained in and through communicative practices. Notably, however, gossip has been absent in CCO thinking and theorizing, despite its prominence as a field that is 'growing in scholarly significance' (Koschmann & Campbell, 2019, p. 174), and the premise that:

> CCO scholarship should be as inclusive as possible about what we mean by (organizational) communication. ... In short, CCO scholars tend to be ecumenical in conceiving of communication, as long as the aim moves beyond investigating talk occurring within an organizational container. (Cooren et al., 2011, pp. 1151–1152)

There is now some emerging evidence that gossip-related research is finding a theoretical footing in CCO scholarship. For example, Fan et al. (2020) argue that their research into 'confidential gossip' and organizational practices where 'gossip and secrecy overlap' (p. 10) makes a distinctive contribution to the CCO field. There is clearly scope for future research into gossip and organizations from this theoretical standpoint, as well as from other theoretical directions. For instance, Ellwardt et al. (2012) also reject the view of gossip as simply the transmission of information inside organizations, arguing that it is useful to think of gossip as a group process. And if this book achieves its aim to help readers to navigate new scholarly terrains, fresh thinking and theoretical developments that begin from a qualitative research starting point are possible.

Qualitative research: a different starting point

Qualitative research is often described in contrasting terms to quantitative research, which is still the dominant paradigm in social sciences and business research (Eriksson & Kovalainen, 2016). However, as Cassell et al. (2018) demonstrate, there is now increasing interest in qualitative research in business and management research. Anderson and Middleton's (2015) analysis of empirical and rhetorical/critical scholarship in communication found that 11% of published articles in prominent communication journals were qualitative. While this may not seem like a lot, it represents over a 100% increase in a 60-year period (Tracy, 2020). The direction and end points of qualitative studies may differ, depending upon the underpinning discipline, theoretical perspective, and research question/s. What qualitative studies offer is the opportunity to extend the breadth and range of inquiry, and elaboration, enhancement, and clarification of the results of quantitative studies (Benoit & Holbert, 2008).

Henderson (2014) argues that research into gossip also has the potential to *disrupt* 'taken-for-granted' traditional qualitative research methods. This, she argues, heralds 'methodology to come ... where researchers actively seek radically different qualitative research methods' (p. 823). From a theoretical standpoint, qualitative research in an emergent field of inquiry, such as gossip, provides an opportunity to critique and extend extant theory. It also provides an opportunity to *build new theory* by attending to 'data that do not easily fit into already developed frameworks' (Tracy, 2020, p. 84, emphasis added). The crucial point here is the need to create complementary methodological and theoretical directions in the field, rather than trying to squeeze gossip into narrow, predetermined designs and conceptual containers. The latter is, metaphorically, like trying to 'nail jelly to a tree' (Waddington, 2010, p. 318); such is the complexity of gossip; or, as the cultural anthropologist Besnier (2019, p. 107, emphasis added) states in a more scholarly manner:

> The mutual constitution of gossip and the private demonstrates that the *private*, as well as its *counterpart the public*, is not a place, a sphere of activity, or a kind of relationship. Rather, it is a *discursive phenomenon* ... it means nothing without *context*. ... It is this semiotic complexity that bestows on it its *slippery quality*.

The elusive and slippery nature of gossip suggests it can be linked with the turn towards post-qualitative inquiry, which proposes that 'meaning and material do not have a fixed nature with strict boundaries but instead which are always in the process of becoming' (Tracy, 2020, p. 43). These issues are addressed in greater depth in Chapter 3: 'Research methods and practices'. However, conceptual confusion in the field of research into gossip in the workplace, and the contested problem of definition, present challenges for researchers and are considered next.

Researching gossip: problems and practice

Michelson et al. (2010) contend that researchers face three major challenges relating to: (i) ethical and moral considerations; (ii) methodological issues; and (iii) the contested problem of definition. They argue that approaches to defining gossip should allow for some *degree of flexibility*:

> By which we mean that agreement should be reached in a general way among scholars as to what are the core elements of gossip so that some accumulation of research findings can occur across studies. (p. 378)

They argue that by identifying the minimum criteria of (i) evaluative talk (written or spoken); (ii) between at least two people; and (iii) about an absent third person/s, it is possible to develop these in a *more nuanced* way, for instance, when studying gossip in different contexts, such as virtual spaces (Gabriels & De Backer, 2016); or from different perspectives, such as the researcher's in autoethnographic research studies (Darmon, 2018); or the work group (Ellwardt et al., 2012). While an enduring challenge for researchers will be one of finding ways through this complex field and publishing their findings, signposts for future research are evident.

Signposts for future research directions

Dores Cruz et al.'s (2021) systematic review suggests a lack of conceptual clarity remains, but they offer a 'broad, integrative definition of gossip: *a sender communicating to a receiver about a target who is absent or unaware of the content*' (p. 275). Their review of 324 articles and associated definitions are thorough, but the concluding definition arguably still reflects the 'organization-as-container' metaphor inside which communication 'happens'. While it is the individual who gossips (with and about other/s), organizations and workplaces/spaces (both actual and virtual) provide the *context and content*. It is crucial that future research does not focus *solely* upon behavioural and interpersonal dimensions of gossip. This is like embarking upon a journey and only seeing what is on the path in front of your feet, and not noticing or appreciating the wider landscape. In the field of mathematics, Dyson (2009) used the analogy of frogs and birds. Some mathematicians are birds, flying high in the sky, surveying vistas out to the far horizon, and delighting in 'concepts that unify our thinking and bring together diverse problems from different parts of the landscape' (p. 212). Others are frogs, living in the mud and seeing only the flowers that grow nearby. The evolving scholarship of organizational gossip needs *both* frog's-eye *and* bird's-eye vantage points, which will involve working at the empirical intersections of qualitative and quantitative research (Benoit & Holbert, 2008).

The new research field of organizational gossip is thus, like many other fields such as international studies, 'one field, many perspectives' (Hermann, 1998, p. 605), and there are some essential transferrable insights. Of note is her argument that we need to trust:

> The inherent intellectual curiosity of those pursuing research ... and their willingness to wrestle with, and not instantly condemn, information that may call some of what they believe into question. (p. 619)

This openness to multiple perspectives creates a foundation for interdisciplinary dialogue and disruption, which Henderson (2014) likens to 'entering a crack', disturbing the taken-for-granted, opening that which might not otherwise be revealed, and creating something new. Drawing upon the philosophical and psychoanalytic work of Deleuze and Guattari, she goes on to argue that a crack refuses to follow familiar rigid molar lines of thought, which produce and reinforce binaries and normative categories, but 'the crack is an in-between space that is always already coming undone' (p. 824). This is a reflection of the conceptual complexity of gossip, and in practical terms, what this means for future research is summarized in Practice Point 1.1.

Practice Point 1.1

Researching in a conceptually complex field

- Seek new ways of approaching definitions, concepts, and methods.
- Work with broad interdisciplinary principles rather than rigid disciplinary practices.
- Acknowledge and become comfortable with uncertainty paradox and contradiction.
- Include ethical reflexivity as an essential aspect of all research designs.

What follows now is a reflexive note on mapmaking, which sets out the epistemological positioning of gossip's contribution to knowledge, and my position and preferences as a 'mapmaker' and reflexive researcher.

A reflexive note on mapmaking

The aim of this book is to provide an expert map of gossip, organization, and work. Like gossip, mapmaking is an old and ubiquitous human impulse and form of communication. A map is a geo/graphical representation of an environment, and also a powerful metaphor to convey ideas of clarification, coherence, and plotting information on paper (Kvernbekk & Jarning, 2019). Maps are significant because they communicate outlines, contours, connections, centres, peripheries, nearness, distance, and boundaries. Importantly, boundaries can connect, divide, and be blurred. They are drawn not only to delineate outside from inside but also to illustrate finer distinctions and details inside the boundary. This requires a 'landscape that allows mapping, that is stable enough to allow the boundaries to make sense' (Kvernbekk & Jarning, 2019, p. 573). The landscape of organizational gossip is emerging as one that is – paradoxically perhaps – stable, with well-established disciplinary boundaries that make sense, yet also uncharted and in need of new pathways and directions to respond to global changes and challenges. Epistemologically, Adkins (2017, p. 3) asserts that 'gossip is a pathway to knowledge', which I extend into the proposition that:

- *Gossip, as a communicative practice and process, is a pathway to organizational knowledge.*

This is a core theme, which I return to and develop throughout the book.

My reflexive position

I know and can navigate the landscape of research in organizational gossip. I may also enter into epistemological spaces with limited knowledge; such is the size, scope, and scale of the field. My reflexive position as a mapmaker is not without its shortcomings. It may be over-reliant on my practitioner-based empirical research, and preference for qualitative and mixed-methods research paradigms. My experience of working in healthcare and higher education, and my 'home' discipline and identity in work psychology have also played a part. Experience and engagement with these empirical materials and disciplinary lenses have helped me to better understand gossip, organizations, and work. But I also experience feelings of frustration when I read academic articles filled with acronyms, and concepts reduced to 2 × 2 matrices and other diagrammatic representations and models (e.g., Lee & Barnes, 2021). I find it difficult to reconcile reading this type of material, no matter how rigorous and scholarly, with the messy reality of organizations and work. When writing, I try where possible to avoid the gratuitously complex language that can creep into academic texts. I'm also curious to explore further the potential of arts-based research and creative theorizing in order to better understand the 'changing picture' of organizational gossip.

Organizational gossip: a changing picture

The term 'changing picture' is deliberately chosen for three reasons. Firstly, it allows for exploration of the phenomenon of gossip that includes *pictorial and visual* elements:

> Gossip is evaluative talk between minimally two people that may be spoken, written [*e.g.,* graffiti, *anonymous memos, emails, text messages, entries and chat on social media*], or visual [*e.g., gestures and looks*]. (van Iterson et al., 2010, p. 378, emphasis added)

The pictorial and visual elements of gossip offer an innovative lens through which to 'see' gossip in a different light, particularly in regard to its role in organizational culture, which, as van Iterson et al. note, has been relatively silent (or perhaps silenced?) in the literature. The second reason for including pictorial and visual elements is to enable us to rethink the 'art and science of gossip' from an academic-practitioner perspective.

The art and science of gossip

Waddington (2020) explores the art and science of gossip, arguing that government-led inquiries/investigations – as discussed above – point to the need to rethink evidence-based management in healthcare. Evidence-based management practice incorporates: (i) use of scientific principles in decisions and management processes; (ii) systematic attention to organizational facts; (iii) advancements in practitioner judgement through critical thinking and decision aids; and (iv) ethical considerations including effects on stakeholders. In essence, this represents 'a product of the distinct yet independent activities of practitioners, educators, and, scholars' (Rousseau, 2012, p. 3). The term 'gossip' has suffered from adverse stereotypical/pejorative assumptions which, until relatively recently, have kept it in the background of scientific research, practitioner judgements, and systematic attention as a form of organizational knowledge and communication. However, the experience and critical thinking of a consultant paediatrician, who is also a designated doctor for child protection and safeguarding children in the UK, offers fresh insights from a practitioner perspective:

> The term gossip has negative connotations, but it can be re-framed as 'useful data'. The *art of using gossip as useful data* will be in receiving it with an open mind. If recurring and from several sources, be curious and interrogate the information being shared. It may be useful in giving

early indications of what is good in the system but also what is not going well that needs addressing before it becomes a serious/significant incident. (Waddington, 2020, p. 20)

I contend the above insights extend beyond healthcare organizations, leading to the final reason for including pictorial and visual elements, which is to explore further the potential of arts-based research practice to bridge the art/science divide (e.g., see Eriksson & Kovalainen, 2016; Leavy, 2020; Plakoyiannaki & Stavraki, 2018). This can create innovative ways of researching and revealing the complex and elusive phenomenon of organizational gossip, for example, by rethinking the relationship between art and gossip.

Art and gossip

Gossip is elusive because it often occurs behind hands, and behind closed doors, whether those doors are 'material' or 'virtual' (Bailenson, 2021; Noon & Delbridge, 1993; Waddington, 2005), richly illustrated in the Belgian artist Pol Ledent's painting *Gossip* depicted in Figure 1.1.

Figure 1.1 vividly challenges the stereotypical imagery of gossip, which frequently represents (white) men and women dressed in business attire exchanging gossip around a water cooler, or as a trivial talk between women. *Gossip* illustrates the concepts of power and emotion. The original artwork is painted in predominantly dark browns, ochre, black, and cream colours, leading us to think that this gossip is more serious, more important. This is no light-hearted, informal 'water cooler moment' or idle 'women's talk' (Fayard & Weekes, 2007; Tebbutt, 1995). We are tasked with guessing, deciphering, and analyzing what we see. For example, the men's clothes could be located in the last hundred years – or more – in continental Europe. Their faces, especially the one receiving the gossip, do not express glee or conspiratorial smugness associated with the popular stereotypes/images of gossip. Quite the opposite in fact; there is a hint of anxiety and tension in his expression. This is not inconsequential chat at the expense of other people to lighten up the day; this gossip is not a trivial pursuit. It contains a cautious note, perhaps a warning? The painting is dark, rough and we can surmise that it lends more weight to the serious type of gossip being shared, and as such gives context to a male world of gossip. The artwork in Figure 1.1 is to some extent a timeless piece, not just by its title *Gossip*, but also by its execution. So, while research into gossip, organization, and work may be an idea whose time has come, the idea of gossip is arguably timeless.

Figure 1.1 Gossip. Source: www.ledent-gallery.be (reproduced with permission).

Conclusion: gossip then and now

The chapter concludes with a brief consideration of the history of gossip in academia, and its parallels with the research process. Gossip spread throughout the 17th and 18th centuries in English coffee house culture. White (2018) notes that the first purpose-built English coffee houses were established in the 1650s in Oxford, where the mind-stimulating bene-fits of coffee complemented the spirit of sober academic discussion and debate at the university. These early coffee houses were christened 'Penny Universities', seen largely as the exclusive resort of the educated and rich;

places where learned men (there is sparse evidence of women attending coffee houses) and their students came to demonstrate their wit and intellectual talents. Here then – historically – the roots of research, in the form of philosophical and scientific discussions, took hold and flourished; and as Ayim later observed (1994, pp. 87–89), there are clear parallels to be drawn between science, research, and gossip:

> The good scientist, as described in the work of Charles Sanders Peirce, will be likely to start with a hunch. … The competent scientist, like the good investigative gossiper, will sift through the plethora of data generated in this listening stance and amend, embrace, or reject the hypothesis accordingly.

While some readers may consider Ayim's parallels between science, research, and gossip to be a little tenuous, there is little doubt that researchers work in teams. This can range from small doctoral supervisory teams to larger inter/national research groups and collaborations. And there is clear evidence of the role that gossip plays in teams regarding group processes and dynamics, feelings of belonging (or not) and bonding, information exchange, and emotional venting (Beersma et al., 2019; Ellwardt et al., 2012). As Beersma et al. note, 'groups are a *breeding ground for gossip*' (p. 417, emphasis added). Therefore researchers, research groups and teams, doctoral students, and their supervisors, may not be 'immune to gossip'. This is something that researchers in the field, whatever their methodological approach and paradigm preference, might usefully, and critically, reflect upon regarding their experiences of gossip.

This chapter has foregrounded organizational gossip as a research phenomenon, provided a brief historical context, and introduced new thinking about the role of arts-based research practice, and post-qualitative enquiry. Next, Chapter 2 addresses key literature and theories in the interdisciplinary scholarship of gossip, and the creative concept of theorizing with art.

Acknowledgement

I would like to thank Hannele Weir for permission to use her interpretation and comments on Pol Ledent's painting *Gossip*, which have deepened my understanding and appreciation of arts-based research and scholarship.

References

Adkins, K. (2017). *Gossip, epistemology, and power: Knowledge underground.* Cham: Palgrave Macmillan/Springer.

Anderson, J. A., & Middleton, M. K. (2015). Epistemological movements in communication: An analysis of empirical and rhetorical/critical scholarship. In P. J. Gehrke, & W. M Keith (Eds.), *A century of communication studies: The unfinished conversation* (pp. 82–108). New York: Routledge.

Ayim, M. (1994). Knowledge through the grapevine: Gossip as inquiry. In R. F. Goodman, & A. Ben-Ze'ev (Eds.), *Good gossip* (pp. 85–99). Kansas, KS: University Press of Kansas.

Bailenson, J. N. (2021). Nonverbal overload: A theoretical argument for the causes of zoom fatigue. *Technology, Mind and Behaviour, 2*(1), [online]. Available at: 10.1037/tmb0000030 [Accessed 31 May 2021].

Beersma, B., Van Kleef, G. A., & Dijkstra, M. T. M. (2019). Antecedents and consequences of gossip in work groups. In F. Giardini, & R. Wittek (Eds.), *The Oxford handbook of gossip and reputation* (pp. 417–434). New York: Oxford University Press.

Benoit, W. L., & Holbert, R. L. (2008). Empirical intersections in communication research: Replication, multiple quantitative methods, and bridging the quantitative–qualitative divide. *Journal of Communication, 58*, 615–628. doi: 10.1111/j.1460-2466.2008.00404.x

Besnier, N. (2019). Gossip in ethnographic perspective. In F. Giardini, & R. Wittek (Eds.), *The Oxford handbook of gossip and reputation* (pp. 100–116). New York: Oxford University Press.

Cassell, C., Cunliffe, A. L., & Grandy, G. (Eds.) (2018). *The SAGE handbook of qualitative business and management research methods.* London: SAGE Publications.

Cole, T. (2006). *Report of the inquiry into certain Australian companies in relation to the UN oil-for-food programme* [online]. Available at: https://apo.org.au/node /3765 [Accessed 6 June 2021].

Cooren, F., Kuhn, T., Cornelissen, J. P., & Clark, T. (2011). Communication, organizing and organization: An overview and introduction to the special issue. *Organization Studies, 32*(9), 114901170. doi: 10.1177/0170840611410836

Darmon, D. J. (2018). Researching the mechanisms of gossip: From fly on the wall to fly in the soup. *Qualitative Report, 23*(7), 1736–1751. doi: 1046743/2160-3715/2018.2912

Dewe, P., & Cooper, C. (2021). *Work and stress: A research overview.* Abingdon: Routledge.

Dores Cruz, T. D., Nieper, A. S., Testori, M., Martinescu, E., & Beersma, B. (2021). An integrative definition and framework to study gossip. *Group & Organization Management, 46*(2), 252–285. doi: 10.1177/1059601121992887

Dyson, F. (2009). Birds and frogs. *Notices of the AMS* [online]. Available at: http:// www.uvm.edu/pdodds/files/papers/others/2009/dyson2009a.pdf [Accessed 31 May 2021].

Ellwardt, L., Labianca, G., & Wittek, R. (2012). Who are the objects of positive and negative gossip at work? A social network perspective on workplace gossip. *Social Networks, 34*(2), 193–205. doi: 10.1016/j.socnet.2011.11.003

Eriksson, P., & Kovalainen, A. (Eds). (2016) *Qualitative methods in business research* (2nd ed.) London: SAGE Publications.

Fan, Z., Grey, C., & Kärreman, D. (2020). Confidential gossip and organization studies. *Organization Studies*, 1–14, [online]. Available at: 10.1177/0170840620954016 [Accessed 31 May 2021].

Fayard, A. L., & Weekes, J. (2007). Photocopiers and water-coolers: The affordances of informal interaction. *Organization Studies*, *28*(05), 605–634. doi: 10.1177/0170840606068310

Fletcher, P. (2009). Narrative painting and visual gossip at the early-twentieth-century Royal Academy. *Oxford Art Journal*, *32*(2), 243–262. doi: 10.1093/oxartj/kcp018

Gabriels, K., & De Backer, C. J. S. (2016). Virtual gossip: How gossip regulates moral life in virtual worlds. *Computers in Human Behavior*, *63*, 683–693. doi: 10.1016/j.chb.2016.05.065

Grant, D., & Nyberg, D. (2011). The view from organizational studies: A discourse-based understanding of corporate social responsibility and communication. In Ø. Ihlen, J. L. Bartlett, & S. May (Eds.), *The handbook of communication and corporate social responsibility* (pp, 534–549). Chichester: John Wiley & Sons.

Hallett, T., Harger, B., & Eder, D. (2009). Gossip at work: Unsanctioned evaluative talk in formal school meetings. *Journal of Contemporary Ethnography*, *38*(5), 584–618. doi: 10.1177/0891241609342117

Henderson, L. (2014). Entering a crack: An encounter with gossip. *International Journal of Qualitative Studies in Education*, *27*(7), 823–836. doi: 10.1080/09518398.2013.820861

Hermann, M. G. (1998). One field, many perspectives: Building the foundations for dialogue. *International Studies Quarterly*, *42*, 605–624. doi: 10.1111/0020-8833.00099

HM Government. (2005). *The Kerr/Haslam Inquiry* [online]. Available at: https://assets.publishing.service.gov.uk/government/uploads/system/uploads/attachment_data/file/273245/6640.pdf [Accessed 31 May 2021].

Kewell, B. (2007). Linking risk and reputation: A research agenda and methodological analysis. *Risk Management*, *9*, 238–254. doi: 10.1057/palgrave.rm.8250029

Koschmann, M. A., & Campbell, T. J. (2019). A critical review of how communication scholarship is represented in textbooks: The case of organizational communication and CCO theory. *Annals of the International Communication Association*, *43*(2), 173–191. doi: 10.1080/23808985.2019.1590785

Kvernbekk, T., & Jarning, H. (2019). Mapping: Coming to grips with educational landscapes. *European Educational Research Journal*, *18*(5) 559–575. doi: 10.1177/1474904119840181

Leavy, P. (2020). *Method meets art: Arts-based research practice*. New York: The Guildford Press.

Lee, S. H., & Barnes, C. M. (2021). An attributional process model of workplace gossip. *Journal of Applied Psychology*, *106*(2), 300–316. doi: 10.1037/apl0000504

Martin, N. (2014). Literature and gossip: An introduction. *Forum for Modern Language Studies*, *50*(2), 135–141. doi: 10.1093/fmls/cqu017

Martinescu, E., Jannsen, O., & Nijstad, B. A. (2019). Gossip and emotion. In F. Giardini, & R. Wittek (Eds.), *The Oxford handbook of gossip and reputation* (pp. 152–169). New York: Oxford University Press.

McAndrew, F. T. (2019). Gossip as a social skill. In F. Giardini, & R. Wittek (Eds.), *The Oxford handbook of gossip and reputation* (pp. 173–192). New York: Oxford University Press.

Meyer, B. H., Prescott, B., & Sheng, X. S. (2021). The impact of the COVID-19 pandemic on business expectations. *International Journal of Forecasting* [online]. Available at: 10.1016/j.ijforecast.2021.02.009 [Accessed 31 May 2021].

Michelson, G., van Iterson, A., & Waddington, K. (2010). Gossip in organizations: Contexts, consequences, and controversies. *Group & Organization Management*, *35*(4), 371–390. doi: 10.1177/1059601109360389

Noon, M., & Delbridge, R. (1993). News from behind my hand: Gossip in organizations. *Organization Studies*, *14*(1), 23–36. doi: 10.1177/017084069301400103

Norris, E., & Shepheard, M. (2017). *How public inquiries can lead to change.* Institute for Government, [online]. Available at: https://www.instituteforgovernment.org.uk/sites/default/files/publications/Public%20Inquiries%20%28final%29.pdf [Accessed 31 May 2021].

O'Connor, N., Kotze, B., & Storm, V. (2018). What's to be done when 'foul whisperings are abroad'? Gossip and rumour in health organisations. *Australasian Psychiatry*, *26*(1), 30–33. doi: 10.1177/1039856217716292

Plakoyiannaki, E., & Stavraki, G. (2018). Collage visual data: Pathways to data analysis. In C. Cassell, A. L. Cunliffe, & G. Grandy (Eds.), *The SAGE handbook of qualitative business and management research methods* (pp. 313–328). London: SAGE Publications.

Reitz, M., & Higgins, J. (2019). *Speak up.* Harlow: Pearson.

Robb, G. (1997). *Victor Hugo.* London: Picador.

Rousseau, D. (2012). Envisioning evidence-based management. In D. Rousseau (Ed.), *The Oxford handbook of evidence-based management.* Oxford: Oxford University Press.

Spreitzer, G. M., Cameron, L., & Garrett, L. (2017). Alternative work arrangements: Two images of the new world of work. *Annual Review of Organizational Psychology and Organizational Behavior*, *4*, 473–99. doi: 10.1146/annurev-orgpsych032516-113332

Tebbutt, M. (1995). *Women's talk? A social history of 'gossip' in working-class neighbourhoods, 1880–1960.* Aldershot: Scolar Press.

Tracy, S. J. (2020). *Qualitative research methods: Collecting evidence, crafting analysis, communicating impact* (2nd ed.) Hoboken, NJ: John Wiley & Sons.

van Iterson, A., & Clegg, S. R. (2008). The politics of gossip and denial in interorganizational relations. *Human Relations*, *61*(8), 1117–1137. doi: 10.1177/0018726708094862

van Iterson, A., Waddington, K., & Michelson, G. (2010). Breaking the silence: The role of gossip in organizational culture. In N. M. Ashkanasay, C. P. M. Wilderom, & M. F. Petersen (Eds.), *Handbook of organizational culture and climate* (2nd ed., pp. 375–392). Thousand Oaks, CA: SAGE Publications.

Waddington, K. (2005). Behind closed doors – The role of gossip in the emotional labour of nursing work. *International Journal of Work Organisation and Emotion, 1*(1), 1–10. doi: 10.1504/IJWOE/2005.007325

Waddington, K. (2010). Organizational gossip, sense-making and the spook fish: A reflexive account. *International Journal of Management Concepts and Philosophy, 4*(3/4), 311–325. doi: 10.1504/IJMCP.2010.037815

Waddington, K. (2012). *Gossip and organization.* Abingdon: Routledge.

Waddington, K. (2016). Rethinking gossip and scandal in healthcare organizations. *Journal of Health Organization and Management, 30*(6), 810–817. doi: 10.1108/JHOM-03-2016-0053

Waddington, K. (2020). The art and science of gossip: Rethinking evidence-based management in healthcare. *Healthcare Transformers* [online]. Available at: https://healthcaretransformers.com/healthcare-business/gossip-evidence-based-management-healthcare/ [Accessed 1 July 2021].

Waddington, K., & Fletcher, C. (2005). Gossip and emotion in nursing and health-care organisations. *Journal of Health, Organization and Management, 19*(4/5), 378–394. doi: 10.1108/14777260510615404

Weick, K. E. (1996). Drop your tools: An allegory for organizational studies. *Administrative Science Quarterly, 41*(2), 301–313. doi: 10.2307/2393722

White, M. (2018). Newspapers, gossip and coffee-house culture. *British Library,* [online]. Available at: https://www.bl.uk/restoration-18th-century-literature/articles/newspapers-gossip-and-coffee-house-culture# [Accessed 17 July 2021].

2 Key literature and theoretical perspectives

Introduction

This chapter addresses the question: what key literature and theoretical perspectives form the foundations for future theorizing on gossip, organization, and work? It lightly traces the theoretical foundations of research and scholarship in the following areas:

- Interdisciplinary foundations of gossip in the social and organizational sciences.
- Relevant strands of critical management studies (CMS) on discourse and narrative.
- Theorizing gossip as organizational communication and knowledge; using art in the theorizing process.

The aim is to offer selected theoretical directions, but the chapter does not (and cannot, in a shortform book such as this) provide a comprehensive summary of current shape of theory in the field. Rather, the intention is to point to novel directions in the process of theorizing gossip. Thus, the chapter is a focused review, which aims to explore a rich range of past and present literature in order to explore the future. It critiques and synthesizes '*representative* literature on [organizational gossip] in an integrated way such that *new frameworks and perspectives* on the topic are generated' (Torraco, 2016: 404, emphasis added). The intention is to offer new ways of attending to, thinking about and theorizing gossip, organization and work. Importantly, the phenomenon of gossip is foregrounded and positioned as organizational knowledge and communication, rather than as simply interpersonal interaction/relationship, for example, between the classic gossip triad of 'sender, receiver and target of gossip' (Bergmann, 1993). Undoubtedly Bergmann's work, inspired by a Simmelian sociological analysis, provides a fundamental social structure and process for gossip.

DOI: 10.4324/9780367652982-2

However, as outlined in Chapter 1, a central theme and argument in this book is that gossip as a communicative practice and process is a pathway to organizational knowledge (Adkins, 2017; Waddington, 2012). First, the interdisciplinary theoretical foundations of gossip are set out in order to lay the ground for this pathway. When making a pathway in the 'real world' there are two key questions to consider:

1. What will be its purpose?
2. Will the land on which it is laid match that purpose, or can it be accordingly restructured?

The (metaphorical) point here is that the current interdisciplinary landscape of gossip needs to be reinterpreted, and conceptually repurposed towards new literatures and theoretical perspectives.

Theoretical foundations of gossip

The theoretical foundations of gossip are dispersed across anthropology, psychology, sociology, social history, linguistics, and philosophy, as well as other disciplines including evolutionary studies. Linguistically, the term 'gossip' originated from the Old English phrase 'godsibb' meaning kinsman or related; Middle English removed the 'd' and 'gossib' took on the meaning of godparent, drinking companion or 'being a friend of' (Ben-Ze'ev, 1994, p. 15). The term was also used to describe the woman who attended birth with a midwife and who subsequently disseminated the news to others. The Middle Ages were a particularly gossipy time, and censure of gossip flourished. The meaning of the word shifted from its positive connotations of female friendship to the negative one of malignant speech and tainted talk. Schein (1994) suggests that the structure of medieval society, with its dependence upon oral communication for news and strict codes of conduct, was an important determining factor in both the prevalence and censure of gossip at that time. There is also a longer history of gossip, which extends back to the politics of reputation and conversations that took place in the open political and social space of the ancient Greek *Agora* in Athens (Gottesman, 2014).

Scholars from a range of disciplines, particularly anthropology and psychology, have pointed to the important role of gossip in the evolution of human language and social behaviour (e.g., Boehm, 2019; Dunbar, 1996; 2004; Hess & Hagen, 2019). Nevertheless, it is difficult to produce a detached, scientific definition of gossip, not only because of the historical negative connotations, but also as it is an elusive activity and a phenomenon that is difficult to define precisely. Further difficulties in defining gossip

Table 2.1 Examples of scholarly definitions of gossip over time

Definition	Insights	Source
Informal communication, which serves to protect individual interests	Anthropological perspective, individual rather than social function	Paine (1967)
News about the affairs of others, or any hearsay of a personal nature	Social psychology perspective, includes reference to self-disclosure	Fine & Rosnow (1978)
Evaluative talk about a person who is not present	Sociological perspective with narrow parameters	Eder & Enke (1991)
Verbal and/or written communication with no obvious conscious purpose regarding the personal matters of a third party	Psychological perspective, gossip as social action	Nevo et al. (1994)
Talk between two or more persons about the private life of another behind that person's back	Emphasizes the secretive and potentially harmful nature of gossip	Taylor (1994)
Idle relaxing activity, value lies in the activity itself, not the outcome	Philosophical perspective, emphasis upon process rather than outcome	Ben-Ze'ev (1994)
The exchange of information about other people/social matters	Evolutionary psychology perspective, broad parameters	Dunbar (1996, 2004)
Informal communication transmitted to others irrespective of whether or not the content is factual	Conceptual study which uses gossip and rumour interchangeably	Michelson & Mouly (2000)
The act of sharing stories with others	Focus upon organizational gossip and storytelling	Gabriel (1995, 2000)
Exchange of personal information in an evaluative way about absent third parties	Inclusive definition set in a context of congeniality, including both positive and negative aspects	Foster (2004)
Evaluative social talk about absent persons, arising in the context of social networks	Functions relate to entertainment, group membership, solidarity, norms, and power structure	DiFonzo & Bordia (2007)
Evaluative talk between at least two persons that is spoken, written, or visual	Multi-perspective approach, draws attention to non-verbal aspects of gossip	van Iterson et al. (2011)
Simultaneously generative, creative communication, and destructive discourse	Philosophical perspective with broad parameters, draws on the linguistic origins of gossip	Adkins (2017)
A sender communicating to a receiver about a target who is absent/unaware of the content	Focus is on the 'gossip triad' and 'organization as container' of communication metaphor	Dores Cruz et al. (2021)

occur as it is closely related to other forms of organizational discourse, such as myths, stories, rumour, small talk, chatting, and urban legends. The conventional differentiation between gossip and rumour is that the latter is usually unverified information about ambiguous or threatening events or situations rather than people (Adkins, 2017). However, the meanings of these different types of organizational discourse such as rumour, myths, stories, and urban legends have merged, multiplied, overlapped and divided. Table 2.1 provides examples of scholarly definitions of gossip over time across disciplinary perspectives.

Table 2.1 illustrates ways how gossip has been conceptualized and defined in diverse ways in the literature. However, rather than seeing this lack of consensus as 'detrimental to the development of the gossip research field' (Dores Cruz et al., 2021, p. 255), I argue that it opens up opportunities for more creative theorizing. As Swedberg (2014, p. xi) argues, 'opening up theorizing to the arts and to the general creativity of human beings is another way of making it more innovative'. This requires fresh thinking, and a shift away from definitions that simply serve to confine and contain the phenomenon of gossip within narrow – and problematic – parameters and paradigms:

> Some of the inherent problems of studying gossip are found in the American writer E. B. White's observation that analysing humour is like dissecting a frog. Few people are interested and the frog dies. ... Overly academic analyses of gossip and gossiping can result in dead descriptions and disengagement on the part of readers. (Waddington, 2012, p. 15, citing van Iterson et al., 2010)

Attempts to police the field of gossip through definitions are, I suggest, fairly futile. As Gabriel (2018, p. 64) argues, terms, concepts, and so forth should be approached 'not as immutable essences, but as elements of language in action'. Gossip has many variants; it can be concurrently vibrant and vivid, amusing and alluring, dangerous and disorderly. But dissecting gossip for the sake of narrow scientific scrutiny will, I argue, ultimately stifle scholarship in the field. A way forward is to integrate: (a) Adkins's (2017) analysis of gossip as being *simultaneously* generative, creative communication, *and* destructive discourse; with (b) van Iterson et al.'s (2010) analysis of gossip as evaluative talk that may be spoken, written, or *visual*. This integrated analysis offers synergies for future scholarship that can draw upon critical management studies, and arts-based paradigms.

Synergies for future scholarship: gossip as narrative and discourse

Narrative and discourse are key strands of CMS (e.g., Forchtner, 2021; Grant et al., 2009; Mills & Helms Mills, 2016). CMS has been described broadly as 'a loose community of scholars and texts focused on power relations and justice' (Swan, 2017, p. 15). Critiques of the latter meaning of CMS are that it has been/is 'dominated by privileged, white, largely Anglo-Saxon men' (Pullen et al., 2017, p. 3). If this book achieves its intention to promote the creation of 'speak up' cultures, it may go some way to inform Swan's (2017, pp. 31–33) manifesto for intervening in practices of sexism and racism in CMS, which involves:

- Building an archive of experiences to gain more knowledge and evidence.
- White academics working on their ability to 'open up, listen up, and learn from others'.
- CMS scholars individually and collectively examining how practices of knowing, unknowing, and not knowing in regard to racism and colonialism are motivated, deliberate, and self-serving in research and teaching practices.

These are ongoing and important issues, and not just in the CMS field. The scholarship of gossip can potentially uncover narratives and stories of difference, discrimination, and bias in universities and other organizations.

Gossip as narrative and stories

Adkins (2017, p. 64) posits that gossip is 'fundamentally storytelling'. This chimes well with the enduring notion of the unmanaged organization made up of 'secrets, gossip, but above all narratives and stories' (Gabriel, 2018, p. 68). Seeing gossip as 'good stories' then becomes an interpretive framework, telling us 'something important happened, and they give *cues*, nods, or downright shoves in *the direction of its meaning(s)*' (Adkins, 2017, p. 65, emphasis added). This points to the allure of gossip as a type of 'mystery story', which in its simplest sense is engaging with something we don't know the answer to. It links to Ayim's (1994) observation that gossip parallels the research process; and it is also *part of* the research process, as revealed in Latour and Woolgar's (1986) ethnographic studies of laboratory life. Seeing gossip as a mystery story reflects the allure of gossip, because mystery stories allude to a promise of 'more pieces to fit together, more layers of meaning, more to be discovered, more to wonder at' (Monaghan, 2020, p. 41).

Visual – and invisible – gossip

Visual elements of gossip can be extended to evoke and provoke new questions, and develop new arts-based insights (Leavy, 2020). For example, this can be extended to include visual/material artefacts with 'evaluative properties' such as artefacts and materialities that express some assessment or judgement about work. Clichéd mugs and magnets saying things like 'you don't have to be crazy to work here, we'll train you', or 'no trespassing, we're tired of hiding the bodies' are still to be found. Such (im)material artefacts also offer insights into the unmanaged organization, where *landmarks* include visual elements such as graffiti and cartoons, as well as gossip, narratives, and stories (Gabriel, 1995). What is different in 21st-century COVID-inflicted organizations is that these landmarks have now taken on altered forms/positions. The coronavirus pandemic, and consequent emptying of offices, work floors, and organizations, has changed the way that spoken, written, and visual talk takes place across public–private interfaces. For example, a WhatsApp group can be set up without anyone outside the group knowing of its existence. Email exchanges with academic and practitioner colleagues while writing this book indicate:

> People are setting up closed social media groups to share gossip and information that wouldn't be appropriate in a public forum. Practitioners are using WhatsApp to maintain social connections (and gossip) with colleagues. Some have separate accounts for 'work' conversations and others for 'social' conversations that exclude line managers. In our WhatsApp group X told me that Y had been brought in to deal with the problem of Z. (Composite of email extracts – some details have been altered to preserve confidentiality.)

Furthermore, emojis (small digital images/icons used to express an idea/emotion, which are now unofficially celebrated on World Emoji Day on 17 July!) and GIFs (Graphic Interchange Format computer files that contain still/moving images) are an increasingly common feature of visual communication in the workplace (Riordan & Glikson, 2020). Smiley faces, angry faces, thumbs up images, hearts, and so forth are 'emotional flavourings' which with evaluative properties appearing in texts, emails, and 'chat' function of online meetings can be recast as visual 'e-gossip'.

Paradoxically, however, online meetings make it easier to engage in *invisible* 'e-gossip', via mobile phone for example, because this can take place away from the gaze of a laptop/computer camera. In face-to-face meetings it is less easy to conceal such activity. The nature of gossip – constituted as evaluative talk that is spoken, written, or visual – has necessarily changed over time, and will continue to do so. Moving from the political gossip of the Greek *Agora* marketplace outlined above, through the coffee shops and 'Penny Universities' discussed in Chapter 1, to the digital discourse of texts, images, tweets, and blogs of 21st-century life and work.

Gossip as discourse

The field of discourse studies, like gossip, draws on a range of literature including linguistics, philosophy, sociology, anthropology, literary studies, communication studies, and social theory (Grant et al., 2009). Discourses are 'meaning systems anchored in socio-historical time that source and constrain communicating actors simultaneously' (Fairhurst & Cooren, 2018, p. 82). However, the field has, until now, discounted and overlooked gossip, arguably because it lurks in the unmanaged organization, and cast as a form of 'degraded discourse'. In the wider field of organizational theorizing in which discourse studies are located, gossip has not – until relatively recently – registered on the radar of 'privileged principled theorizing and empiricist analysis' (Grant et al., 2009, pp. 227–228). Times are changing, and while it is pleasing to see research and scholarship in the field of gossip emerging, it appears that privileged theorizing and empirical analysis still prevail.

While such studies offer theoretical insights, they are problematic for two reasons. Firstly, experimental studies tend to focus on the negative nature of gossip. In other words, 'if gossip is operationalized as [a warning to] ingoup members about free-riders, it will always pertain to negative gossip' (Farley, 2019, p. 354). Note, this is gossip as a warning about *individual behaviours*, which is quite different to the argument advanced in the book that gossip can act as a warning of *organizational failure*. Secondly, they tend to rely on seeing the gossip triad of sender, receiver, and target, through traditional theoretical and disciplinary lenses, rather than a 'gossip as discourse' lens. For example, although Lee and Barnes's (2021) attributional process model of workplace gossip focuses on the potential *positive* as well as negative consequences for the 'sender', it offers little in the way of *new theorizing*. Future theorizing, I suggest, will benefit from a move away from 'derivative theory' based on existing social/organization science. As Mumby and Putnam (2014, p. 13) comment: 'consistently leaning on the same theoretical crutch has the unfortunate effect of transforming it into a hammer'. Future theorizing must also re-orientate away from the outdated 'organization as container' and 'gossip triad' approaches to connect with contemporary approaches to communication, organization, and organizing. The interdisciplinary landscape of gossip needs to be reinterpreted, and conceptually repurposed, to cover new contours and contexts.

Theorizing gossip: new contours and contexts

This section traces new contours and contexts for theorizing gossip in regard to:

- Epistemological positioning of gossip as organizational knowledge and communication.
- Communicative constitution of organization (CCO) scholarship.

Gossip as organizational knowledge and communication

Here, organizational knowledge *and* organizational communication are seen as a 'both-and' composite, rather than separate 'either/or' entities. This represents the 'communicative *practices* of organizational knowledge' (Canary & McPhee, 2011, p. 8), a practice-based approach that emphasizes the social and interactive nature of knowledge. A practice-based view of organizational knowledge rejects the view of knowledge as an identifiable, and commodifiable, entity. Instead:

> Analytic concern thus turns away from identifying the existence or uniqueness of knowledge, and turns instead to *processes of knowing*, seeing these processes as always embodied, embedded in particular socio-historical settings and communities, and intimately connected to the material factors through which they emerge. (Kuhn & Porter, 2011, p. 18)

The emergent and processual character of organizational knowledge is such that it cannot be neatly commodified and counted; nor can it be 'reduced to a reproducible synoptic pattern' (Tsoukas, 2011, p. xv). Theorizing gossip as organizational knowledge and communication is based on the assumption that 'communication ideas and paths of inquiry are relevant to the concept and phenomenon of organizational knowledge' (McPhee et al., 2011, p. 304). Theorizing gossip as organizational knowledge is also based on the assumption that gossip is an epistemic process.

Gossip as an epistemic process

Bartolutti and Magnani (2019) see gossip as an epistemic process, inherently social in its content and purpose, and contend that its theoretical rehabilitation is indebted to anthropology and cognitive/evolutionary studies. Building upon Ayim's (1994) argument that there are similarities between gossip and Charles Sanders Peirce's pragmatic philosophy of science, gossip is seen as 'making an abduction [everyday reasoning] upon a series of contextual clues' (Ayim, 1994, p. 279). Or, more simply perhaps, by seeing gossip as narrative and stories (as discussed above), this becomes a mystery story – a story driven by curiosity, and an evolutionary and epistemic need to know and fill in information gaps (Monaghan, 2020). Bartolutti and Magnani (2019, p. 274) argue that it is 'fairly obvious' to see organizational gossip as applied social epistemology. This is a field that straddles the boundary between epistemology and ethics, and is characterized by: (i) 'a concern for relevance to the *ordinary affairs of everyday* (non-philosophical) *life*'; and (ii) 'being addressed to an audience [e.g., practitioners] that isn't exclusively philosophical (Chase & Coady, 2019, p. 6, emphasis added).

Importantly, Adkins (2017, p. 52) also contends that the language of applied social epistemology supports the argument that 'gossip as discourse can work as a kind of epistemic imagination'. For Adkins, the contribution that gossip makes to knowledge is most clearly recognized with the context of power relations and imbalances between groups. Power and knowledge are also core concerns of critical management studies (CMS), which adopt a Foucauldian approach, recognizing that power is everywhere – diffused and embodied in discourse and language (Knights, 2009). Gossip as a form of power is well documented in the ethnographic literature, but also hotly contested in regard to its role as a cultural device to promote individual interests, or as a form of social control that promotes unity in groups (Giardini & Wittek, 2019; Gluckman, 1963). While Farley (2019) argues that future research should address the potential power of positive gossip. The key points to be made here are: (i) understanding gossip as a form of power is critical; and (ii) seeing gossip as a communicative process and pathway to organizational knowledge grounds future scholarship in the interdisciplinary field of organizational communication.

Gossip as organizational communication: theoretical perspectives

According to Sotirin (2014), theory holds a privileged position in organizational communication scholarship, which is characterized by eclectic, multi-theoretical perspectives. This is a field with substantial depth and breadth of post-positivism, interpretivism, critical theory, critical realism, and social constructivism, viewed positively and creatively. While anthropology, sociology, social psychology, and cognitive/evolutionary studies have undoubtedly contributed to the rehabilitation of gossip, future theorizing needs to move on now from its disciplinary foundations. The interdisciplinary field of organizational communication, I argue, holds the key to the next stage of its rehabilitation. Organizational communication scholarship is known for 'conceptual borrowing across diverse philosophical and theoretical sources' (Sotirin, 2014, p. 20). A key theme is inclusivity, and inclusion of gossip can only contribute to the breadth of the field. This can bring something unique to the body of knowledge that *elevates communication* from being another organizational phenomenon (or variable) to the means by which 'organizational structures and processes are constituted' (Mumby & Putnam, 2014, p. 4). This is the field of communicative constitution of organization (CCO) thinking and scholarship.

Communicative constitution of organization (CCO) scholarship

CCO scholarship positions communication as the 'main force that creates, generates, and sustains – constitutes – what we consider to be organization and organizing practices' (Schoeneborn et al., 2019, p. 476). Very briefly, there are three main schools of thought:

1. McPhee and Zaug's 'four flows' model comprising: (i) membership negotiation; (ii) organizational self-structuring; (iii) activity co-ordination; and (iv) institutional positioning.
2. Luhmann's social systems theory of communication, which minimizes human agency, and is wholly communicative; an amalgam of information, utterance, and understanding.
3. The Montréal School, which synthesizes multiple lines of research and reflections on the role of language under the rubric of *communication as organizing*.

Schoeneborn et al. (2014) offer a more detailed, systematic comparison of the three schools of CCO thought, while Cooren et al. (2011, pp. 1151–1153) identify six premises to help define more precisely what CCO scholarship entails. These are summarized below, with additional comment regarding what this means for repositioning gossip as organizational knowledge and organizational constitution.

Premise 1: CCO scholarship studies communicational events.
  An event is a segment of an ongoing and situated stream of socio-discursive practice, including any turn of talk, metaphor, artefact, or narrative. Gossip is clearly a stream of socio-discursive practice, which may trickle or surge through organizations, blending and blurring with other

communicative events such as rumour and storytelling as part of a wider family of communicative practices.

Premise 2: CCO scholarship should be as inclusive as possible about what we mean by (organizational) communication.

The majority of work on organizational communication and discourse has ignored gossip, focusing almost exclusively on the *textual* aspects of communication. If CCO scholarship and discourse studies are to be as inclusive as possible, then gossip can no longer be ignored.

Premise 3: CCO scholarship acknowledges the co-constructed or co-oriented nature of (organizational) communication.

A CCO view asks how the meaning and action/s embedded in policies, decisions, or job descriptions, for example, are negotiated, translated, and/or debated.

Premise 4: CCO scholarship holds that who or what is acting is always an open question.

This premise advocates inclusivity regarding *what* or *who* is taking part in the constitution of organizational processes; the *what* includes organizational strategies, visions, mission statements, and so forth, extending the scope of gossip to incorporate topics beyond simply absent third parties.

Premise 5: CCO scholarship never leaves the realm of communicational events.

Contemporary communicative thinking, however, broadens its explanatory reach to consider how the ideational and material – as in those buildings, strategies, statuses, operations, bodies, conversations, art, photographs, and documents – are co-implicated and co-constituted in organizing. This aligns well with the notion of *visual* gossip.

Premise 6: CCO scholarship favours neither organizing nor organization.

CCO scholarship refuses to choose between studying how people get organized and how organizations come to be re-enacted and reproduced through these activities. The slipperiness of gossip as a *process*, *product*, and *person* thus pervades the ongoing scholarship of gossip as CCO thinking and theorizing.

CCO scholarship offers a signpost for future research and theorizing into organizational gossip as a communicative practice and process of knowing. Putnam and Mumby (2014, p. 13) note that *The Montréal School* variant of CCO thinking in organizational communication is 'the primary perspective that originates wholly in our field [with] sophisticated communication-based concepts that focus on the dynamic relationships among conversation, text and organization'. CCO thinking illuminates the relationships between everyday micro-level communication and societal macro-level meaning systems. Thus gossip as everyday micro- and macro-level communication is no longer simply an idea whose time has come (as argued in Chapter 1). It is also arguably an idea that can find a home in future CCO scholarship and thinking. Developing communicative modes of understanding gossip in terms of meaning and sensemaking can reveal previously silent, dynamic, interactional qualities of organizational life and organizational cultures.

Additionally, I contend that an arts-based research paradigm, broadly understood as a flexible architecture of practice-based theory building (Rolling, 2018), can intersect with and augment communicative modes of understanding. In practical terms, what this could look like is summarized in Practice Point 2.1, based on the idea of 'mystery creation' (Alvesson & Sköldberg, 2018, p. 387), and the role of reflexive methodology in creating and crafting new theoretical ideas and knowledge.

Practice Point 2.1

Putting practice into theory
Engage with gossip as a *mystery story from and about practice* and ask:

- What are the assumptions and questions in this story?
- Is it an interesting story?
- What clues does it contain?
- What answers does it offer?
- Are there any unexpected/interesting surprises or twists in the tale?
- What theoretical insights help us to make sense of this story?

The idea of putting practice into theory can lead to imaginative theorizing using arts-based practices, with which the chapter concludes.

Theorizing with art

Arts-based theorizing sits at the intersection of art and science. Physicist Erwin Schrödinger (1887–1961) made an apposite observation on the science–art intersection: 'Thus the task [of science] is not so much to see what no one has yet seen; but to *think what nobody has yet thought* about that which everybody sees' (in Bynum & Porter, 2006, p. 538, emphasis added). Both fields share similarities in their quest to generate representative models that assist in the understanding of human experience. However, statistically expressed, numerical, or linear models and 'conventionally constructed' frameworks can channel thinking along predetermined epistemologies and theories, which can bind and/or blind researchers. This may debilitate the development of new knowledge and thinking, and applies to both quantitative and qualitative research. As Cornelissen (2016, p. 368) comments:

> In recent years qualitative papers are increasingly being fashioned in the image of quantitative research, so much so that papers adopt 'factor-analytic' styles of theorizing that have typically been the preserve of quantitative methods. This is a worrying trend as it leads to certain types of explanations dominating our field.

According to Rolling (2018, pp. 509–510), arts-based theorizing opens up new ways of thinking that involves:

> Learning *analytically* through observation, experience, and/or experimentation, building new forms of procedural and material knowledge; thinking and learning *synthetically*, expressing new information about current and often invisible knowledge [viz. gossip] as represented from a confluence of symbolic languages.

Reflexivity, which involves thinking idiosyncratically across different ways of knowing and doing, rather than being tied to particular conventions, is crucial to arts-based theorizing. While the principles of arts-based theorizing may appear to have more resonance in a qualitative research context, they draw upon Charles Sanders Peirce's pragmatic philosophy, and have wider application to other fields of research. The key message for researchers is to begin theory building by revealing evidence of how you are *making sense of the prevailing discourse(s)* surrounding your research question, rather than simply repeating/rolling out formulaic research designs. What this means in practice is 'simultaneously *making visible* your process of representing its meaningfulness to you' (Rolling, 2018, p. 509).

Making the theorizing process visible

Figure 2.1 is a 'conventionally constructed' theorizing framework based on empirical findings from my own mixed methods (but predominantly qualitative) research into practitioners' and managers' experiences of gossip in nursing and healthcare organizations.

The framework in Figure 2.1 was based on Corley and Gioia's (2011, p. 12) assumption that 'theory is a statement of concepts and their interrelationships that shows how and/or why a phenomenon occurs'. Weick (1979) argues that theorizing should strive not only for generality and abstraction, but that it should also capture relationships and suggest 'evocative images' (p. 26). Figure 2.1 communicates core concepts of

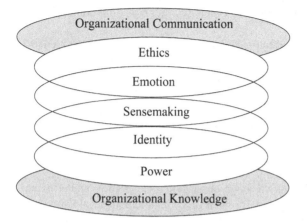

Figure 2.1 Theorizing gossip as organizational communication and knowledge. Source: Waddington (2012, p. 149). Artwork by Hannah Waddington (reproduced with permission).

gossip as organizational knowledge and communication: ethics, emotion, sensemaking, identity, and power. But it does not reflect the messy realities of everyday life and experience of gossip in the workplace. On the other hand, the artwork in Figure 2.2 (reproduced with permission) offers a more visually inspiring image with which to think about theorizing gossip.

Figure 2.2 is taken from Tacita Dean's (1997) work *The Roaring Forties: Seven Boards in Seven Days* (1997), which constructs a narrative of sailors battling storms in an area of the Atlantic known for strong winds. Each of the seven pieces contains diagrammatic arrows and notes that specify atmospheric conditions, wind directions, time, dates, camera angles, and details of narrative incident. The image portrayed in Figure 2.2 is of six men rolling a sail, visually represented as a vertebral structure, which, for me, reflects the core concepts of gossip illustrated in Figure 2.1. It powerfully captures and underscores the intended – but difficult to communicate in a diagrammatic way – the fluidity and movement of the theorizing framework. Tacita Dean's work explores the boundaries between perception and reality, fact and fiction; features which are conceptually relevant to the scholarship of gossip.

The image also has a sense of ambiguity and impermanence, which also reflects the nature and characteristics of gossip. Arts-based theorizing is a powerful way of bringing gossip into the foreground.

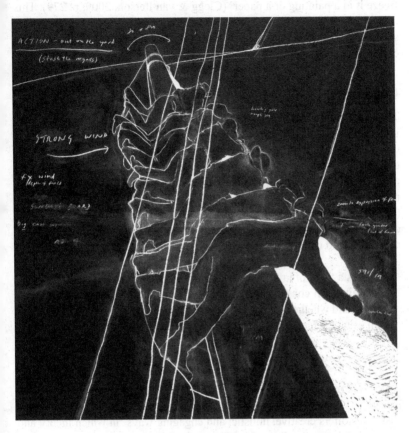

Figure 2.2 The roaring forties: seven boards in seven days. © Tacita Dean 1997.
Source: Courtesy the artist, Frith Street Gallery, London, and Marian
Goodman Gallery, New York/Paris.

Foregrounding gossip with art

Foregrounding and representing gossip as organizational knowledge and
communication – rather than as whisperings behind hands, and behind
doors – allows the 'background' and 'back story/stories' of gossip to be
seen and heard. This also allows for other evocative images to come into
play. For example, Clegg and van Iterson (2009) refer to the cubist-style
painting *Les Demoiselle's d'Avignon* by Picasso (1881–1973), which prob-
lematizes and subverts the established figure–ground hierarchy by placing
equal emphasis on each. 'With Picasso, we see figure and ground as existing in dialectical tension that is constantly in movement – even if we can

freeze it in a painting or a paper' (Clegg & van Iterson, 2009, p. 279). This is an excellent example of ways in which art can be used to cast new understandings, by shifting emphasis and/or perspective to help us make sense of experience and generate meaning (Adkins, 2017).

Conclusion

This chapter has traced the theoretical roots of gossip in the social and organizational sciences, and its positioning in discourse and narrative strands of CMS. These theoretical roots are deep, although there is acknowledgement that CMS is under attack (Huws, 2021; Morrish, 2021). This is largely attributed to the 'status of CMS as an alternative (peripheral) approach in relation to the positivist/functionalist mainstream in the management field' (Bristow et al., 2017, p. 1186). Gossip has also been reorganized as a process of organizational knowledge and communication, and future CMS research could usefully revisit Carr's (2003, p. 8) proposition that:

> Art as a form of knowledge, and having a language-like character, will culminate in considering the forms of rescuing its own critical dimension, and whether similar forms could be used for *critical* management. In using the term 'critical management', I wish to denote forms of thinking that help us see anew that which we have taken-for-granted and may have blinded us to alternative constructions of problems and solutions.

Arts-based research practices also offer a set of methodological tools used by researchers across disciplines during any or all phases of the research process. This offers creative, holistic, and engaging ways 'in which theory and practice are intertwined' (Leavy, 2020, p. 4). This chapter has also argued that communicative constitution of organization (CCO) thinking and theorizing is a promising avenue for future research, although in the first instance gossip may be cast as a fragile form of constitution in this field. I hope that material in this chapter will provide the foundations for a new generation of research and future theorizing. These are broad and deep theoretical and conceptual foundations, which serve to bring gossip from its historical back-stage position as an afterthought, into the foreground of contemporary organizational scholarship. Next, Chapter 3 considers research methods and practices necessary to cultivate and craft a new and emerging research agenda.

References

Adkins, K. (2017). *Gossip, epistemology, and power: Knowledge underground.* Cham: Palgrave Macmillan/Springer.

Alvesson, M., & Sköldberg, K. (2018). *Reflexive methodology: New vistas for qualitative research* (3rd ed.) London: SAGE Publications.

Ayim, M. (1994). Knowledge through the grapevine: Gossip as inquiry. In R. F. Goodman & A. Ben-Ze'ev (Eds.), *Good gossip* (pp. 85–99). Kansas, KS: University Press of Kansas.

Bartolutti, T., & Magnani, L. (2019). Gossip. In D. Coady, & J. Chase (Eds.), *The Routledge handbook of applied epistemology* (pp. 272–283). Abingdon: Routledge.

Ben-Ze'ev, A. (1994). The vindication of gossip. In R. F. Goodman, & A. Ben-Ze'ev (Eds.), *Good gossip* (pp. 11–24). Kansas, KS: University Press of Kansas.

Bergmann, J. R. (1993). *Discreet indiscretions: The social organization of gossip.* New York: Aldine de Gruyter.

Boehm, C. (2019). Gossip and reputation in small-scale societies: A view from evolutionary anthropology. In F. Giardini, & R. Wittek (Eds.), *The Oxford handbook of gossip and reputation* (pp. 253–274). New York: Oxford University Press.

Bristow, A., Robinson, S., & Ratle, O. (2017). Being an early-career CMS academic in the context of insecurity and 'excellence': The dialectics of resistance and compliance. *Organization Studies, 38*(9), 1185–1207. doi: 10.1177/0170840616685361

Bynum, W. F., & Porter, R. (2006). *Oxford dictionary of scientific quotations.* Oxford: Oxford University Press.

Canary, H. E., & McPhee, R. D. (2011). Introduction: Toward a communicative perspective on organizational knowledge. In H. E. Canary, & R. D. McPhee (Eds.), *Communication and organizational knowledge: Contemporary issues for theory and practice* (pp. 1–14). New York: Routledge.

Carr, A. (2003). Art as a form of knowledge: The implications for critical management. In A. Carr & P. Hancock (Eds.), *Art and aesthetics at work* (pp. 7–37). Houndmills: Palgrave Macmillan.

Clegg, S. R., & van Iterson, A. (2009). Dishing the dirt: Gossiping in organizations. *Culture and Organization, 15*(3), 275–289.

Coady, J., & Chase, D. (2019). The return of applied epistemology. In D. Coady, & J. Chase (Eds.), *The Routledge handbook of applied epistemology* (pp. 3–12). Abingdon: Routledge.

Cooren, F., Kuhn, T., Cornelissen, J. P., & Clark, T. (2011). Communication, organizing and organization: An overview and introduction to the special issue. *Organization Studies, 32*(9), 114901170. doi: 10.1177/0170840611410836

Corley, K. G., & Gioia, D. A. (2011). Building theory about theory building: What constitutes a theoretical contribution? *Academy of Management Review, 36*(1), 12–32. doi: 10.5465/amr.2009.0486

Cornelissen, J. P. (2016). Preserving theoretical divergence in management research: Why the explanatory potential of qualitative research should be harnessed rather than supressed. *Journal of Management Studies, 54*(3), 368–383. doi: 10.111/joms.12210

DiFonzo, N., & Bordia, P. (2007). *Rumor psychology: Social and organizational approaches.* Washington, DC: American Psychological Association.

Dores Cruz, T. D., Nieper, A. S., Testori, M., Martinescu, E., & Beersma, B. (2021). An integrative definition and framework to study gossip. *Group & Organization Management, 46*(2), 252–285. doi: 10.1177/1059601121992887

Dunbar, R. (1996). *Grooming, gossip and the evolution of language*. London: Faber & Faber.

Dunbar, R. (2004). Gossip in evolutionary perspective. *Review of General Psychology, 8*(2), 100–110. doi: 10.1037/1089-2680.8.2.100

Eder, D., & Enke, J.L. (1991). The structure of gossip: Opportunities and constraints on collective expression among adolescents. *American Sociological Review, 56*(4), 494–508. doi: 10.2307/2096270

Fairhurst, G. T., & Cooren, F. (2018). Organizational discourse analysis. In C. Cassell, A. L. Cunliffe, & G. Grandy (Eds.), *The SAGE handbook of qualitative business and management research methods* (pp. 82–101). London: SAGE Publications.

Farley, S. (2019). On the nature of gossip, reputation, and power inequality. In F. Giardini, & R. Wittek (Eds.), *The Oxford handbook of gossip and reputation* (pp. 343–358). New York: Oxford University Press.

Fine, G. & Rosnow, R. (1978). Gossip, gossipers, gossiping. *Personality and Social Psychology Bulletin, 4*(1), 161–168. doi: 10.1177/014616727800400135

Forchtner, B. (2021). Introducing 'narrative in critical discourse studies'. *Critical Discourse Studies, 18*(3), 304–313. doi: 10.1080/17405904.2020.1802765

Foster, E.K. (2004). Research on gossip: Taxonomy, methods and future directions. *Review of General Psychology, 8*(2), 78–99. doi: 10.1037/1089-2680.8.2.78

Gabriel, Y. (1995). The unmanaged organization: Stories, fantasies and subjectivity. *Organization Studies, 16*(3), 477–501. doi: 10.1177/017084069501600305

Gabriel, Y. (2000). *Storytelling in organizations: Facts, fictions and fantasies.* Oxford: Oxford University Press.

Gabriel, Y. (2018). Stories and narratives. In C. Cassell, A. L. Cunliffe, & G. Grandy (Eds.), *The SAGE handbook of qualitative business and management research methods* (pp. 63–81). London: SAGE Publications.

Giardi, F., & Wittek, R. (2019). Gossip, reputation, and sustainable cooperation: Sociological foundations. In F. Giardini, & R. Wittek (Eds.), *The Oxford handbook of gossip and reputation* (pp. 23–46). New York: Oxford University Press.

Gluckman, M. (1963). Gossip and scandal. *Current Anthropology, 4*(3), 307–316. doi: 10.1086/200378

Gottesman, A. (2014). *Politics and the street in democratic Athens.* New York: Cambridge University Press.

Grant, D., Iedema, R., & Oswick, C. (2009). Discourse and critical management studies. In M. Alvesson, T. Bridgman, & H. Willmott (Eds.), *The Oxford handbook of critical management studies* (pp. 213–231). Oxford: Oxford University Press.

Hess, N. H., & Hagen, E. H. (2019). Gossip, reputation, and friendship in within-group competition: An evolutionary perspective. In F. Giardini, & R. Wittek (Eds.), *The Oxford handbook of gossip and reputation* (pp. 275–302). New York: Oxford University Press.

Huws, H. (2021). Is critical management studies still welcome in business schools? *Times Higher Education* [online]. Available at: https://www.timeshi ghereducation.com/blog/critical-management-studies-still-welcome-business -schools [Accessed 20 July 2021].

Knights, D. (2009). Power at work in organizations. In M. Alvesson, T. Bridgman, & H. Willmott (Eds.), *The Oxford handbook of critical management studies* (pp. 144–165). Oxford: Oxford University Press.

Kuhn, T., & Porter, A. J. (2011). Heterogeneity in knowledge and knowing: A social practice perspective. In H. E. Canary, & R. D. McPhee (Eds.), *Communication and organizational knowledge: Contemporary issues for theory and practice* (pp. 17–34). New York: Routledge.

Latour, B., & Woolgar, S. (1986). *Laboratory life: The construction of scientific facts*. Princeton, NJ: Princeton University Press.

Leavy, P. (2020). *Method meets art: Arts-based research practice*. New York: The Guildford Press.

Lee, S. H., & Barnes, C. M. (2021). An attributional process model of workplace gossip. *Journal of Applied Psychology, 106*(2), 300–316. doi: 10.1037/ ap10000504

McPhee, R. D., Canary, H. E., & Iverson, J. O. (2011). Conclusion: Moving forward with communicative perspectives on organizational knowledge. In H. E. Canary, & R. D. McPhee (Eds.), *Communication and organizational knowledge: Contemporary issues for theory and practice* (pp. 304–313). New York: Routledge.

Michelson, G., & Mouly, S. (2000). Rumour and gossip in organisations: A conceptual study. *Management and Decision Making, 38*(5), 339–346.

Mills, A. J., & Helms Mills, J. (2016). Critical management scholarship: A satirical critique of three narrative histories. In A. Prasad, P. Prasad, A. J. Mills, & J. Helms Mills (Eds.), *The Routledge companion to critical management studies* (pp. 45–55). Abingdon: Routledge.

Monaghan, E. M. (2020). The allure of mysteries. *The Psychologist, 33*(12), 38–41.

Morrish, L. (2021). Academic freedom is in crisis: Free speech is not. *Council for the Defence of British Universities* [online]. Available at: http://cdbu.org.uk/ academic-freedom-is-in-crisis-free-speech-is-not/ [Accessed 20 July 2021].

Nevo, O., Nevo, B., & Derech-Zehavi, A. (1994). The tendency to gossip as a psychological disposition: Constructing a measure and validating it. In R. F. Goodman, & A. Ben-Ze'ev (Eds.), *Good gossip* (pp. 180–192). Kansas, KS: University Press of Kansas.

Paine, R (1967). What is gossip about? An alternative hypothesis. *Man*, 278–285. doi: 10.2307/2799493

Putnam, L. L., & Mumby, D. K. (2014). Introduction: Advancing theory and research in organizational communication. In L. L. Putnam, & D. K. Mumby (Eds.), *The SAGE handbook of organizational communication: Advances in theory, research and methods* (3rd ed., pp. 1–18). Thousand Oaks, CA: SAGE Publications.

Pullen, A., Harding, N., & Phillips, M. (2017). Introduction: Feminist and queer politics in critical management studies. In A., Pullen, N. Harding, & M. Phillips

(Eds.), *Feminists and queer theorists debate the future of critical management studies* (pp. 1–12). Bingley: Emerald Publishing Limited.

Riordan, M. A., & Glikson, E. (2020). On the hazards of the technology age: How using emojis affects perceptions of leaders. *International Journal of Business Communication* [online]. Available at: 10.1177/2329488420971690 [Accessed 9 Jan 2021].

Rolling, J. R. (2018) Arts-based research in education. In P. Leavy (Ed.), *Handbook of arts-based research* (pp. 493–510). New York: The Guildford Press.

Schein, S. (1994). Used and abused: Gossip in medieval society. In R. F. Goodman, & A. Ben-Ze'ev (Eds.), *Good gossip* (pp. 139–153). Kansas, KS: University Press of Kansas.

Schoeneborn, D., & Blaschke, S., with Cooren, F., McPhee, R. D., Seidl, D., & Taylor, J. R. (2014). The three schools of CCO thinking: Interactive dialogue and systematic comparison. *Management Communication Quarterly*, *28*(2), 285–316. doi: 10.1177/0893318914527000

Schoeneborn, D., Kuhn, T. R., & Kärreman, D. (2019). The communicative constitution of organization, organizing, and organizationality. *Organization Studies*, *40*(4), 475–496. doi: 10.1177/0170840618782284

Sotirin, P. J. (2014). Theories of organizational communication. In L.L. Putnam, & D. K. Mumby (Eds.), *The SAGE handbook of organizational communication: Advances in theory, research and methods* (3rd ed., pp. 19–26). Thousand Oaks, CA: SAGE Publications.

Swan, E. (2017). Manifesto for feminist critical race killjoys in CMS. In A. Pullen, N. Harding, & M. Phillips (Eds.), *Feminists and queer theorists debate the future of critical management studies* (pp. 13–38). Bingley: Emerald Publishing Limited.

Swedberg, R. (2014). Preface. In R. Swedberg (Ed), *Theorizing in social science: The context of discovery* (pp. ix–xvi). Stanford, CA: Stanford University Press.

Taylor, G. (1994). Gossip as moral talk. In R.F. Goodman, & A. Ben-Ze'ev (Eds.), *Good gossip* (pp. 34–46). Kansas, KS: University Press of Kansas.

Torraco, R. J. (2016). Writing integrative literature reviews: Using the past and present to explore the future. *Human Resource Development Review*, *15*(4), 404–428. doi: 10.1177/1534484316671606

Tsoukas, H. (2011). Foreword: Representation, signification, improvisation – A three-dimensional view of organizational knowledge. In H. E. Canary, & R. D. McPhee (Eds.), *Communication and organizational knowledge: Contemporary issues for theory and practice* (pp. x–xix). New York: Routledge.

van Iterson, A., Waddington, K., &, Michelson, G. (2010). Breaking the silence: The role of gossip in organizational culture. In N.M. Ashkanasay, C. P. M. Wilderom, & M. F. Petersen (Eds.), *Handbook of organizational culture and climate* (2nd ed., pp. 375–392). Thousand Oaks, CA: SAGE Publications.

Waddington, K. (2012). *Gossip and organization*. Abingdon: Routledge.

Weick, K. E. (1979). *The social psychology of organizing* (2nd ed.). Reading, MA: Addison-Wesley.

3 Research methods and practices

Introduction: a future-proof, real-world research agenda

The aim of this chapter is to bring an innovative approach to researching gossip as a communicative practice and pathway to organizational knowledge in the changing landscape of organization and work. It is based on the assumption and argument that future research needs to engage with lived – rather than laboratory – experiences of gossip, to ensure it is 'future proof'. This is needed to take the phenomenon of gossip from an *evolving* area of business scholarship into an *enduring* field of research. This field is already well served by organizational, management, and business research texts. For example: Allen (2017) *The SAGE Encyclopedia of Organizational Communication Research Methods*; Bazeley (2019) *A Practical Introduction to Mixed Methods for Business and Management*; Cassell et al. (2018a) *The SAGE Handbook of Qualitative Business and Management Research Methods*; Easterby-Smith et al. (2021) *Management and Business Research* 7th ed; Eriksson and Kovalainen (2016) *Qualitative Methods in Business Research* 2nd ed; Putnam and Mumby (2014) *The SAGE Handbook of Organizational Communication: Advances in Theory, Research and Methods* 3rd ed; Wodak and Meyer (2016) *Methods of Critical Discourse Analysis* 3rd ed.

Methods of studying organizational communication phenomena addressed in the above (and indeed many other research texts) include field studies, surveys, network mapping, interviewing, discourse analysis, and ethnographic approaches. Future research is indebted to the contribution that these methods and approaches have made, and can continue to make, but they are not repeated in detail here. Instead, this chapter discusses how future research into gossip needs to be eclectic, evocative, and imaginative, rather than being constrained to precise, privileged positions and methodologies. Chapter 2 laid out the interdisciplinary foundations, key literature, theories, and approaches to theorizing, and was a necessarily 'heavy' chapter. By which I

DOI: 10.4324/9780367652982-3

mean (metaphorically), rather like a celebratory meal it took time to prepare, and contained a substantial amount of material that will take time to digest. Chapter 2 constitutes what can be seen as 'food for thought'. It included Alvesson and Sköldberg's (2018) reflexive methodology and the notion of mystery creation as staple 'ingredients' for the creation of new theoretical ideas and knowledge. This chapter now invites readers to take a 'break between courses' as it were and take some time to think about future research directions, methods, priorities, and practices. However it does not seek to provide a prescriptive approach; this chapter is not about 'methodological policing'. Rather it makes the case for adapting and advancing organizational communication research methods and considering the contribution of arts-based practice in a thoughtful and reflexive manner. It sets out an ambitious, innovative, and provocative interdisciplinary research agenda. This includes a discussion of the challenges facing researchers who choose to use methods and practices that run counter to conventional and powerful paradigms in business and management research and some pragmatic solutions.

Priorities for future research

There are three priorities for future research. Firstly, it must produce public scholarship with social impact beyond academia, institutional rankings, and individual academic career advancement in narrowly defined and competitive research environments (Arnold et al., 2021). Put simply, future research needs to take place in collaborative and compassionate scholarly environments and cultures (Waddington, 2019, 2021). Such environments and cultures are characterized by 'collective interdisciplinary efforts [that] contrast the individual-level gamesmanship prevalent in academia today' (Breslin, 2021, p. 49). Secondly, Chapter 2 advanced the argument that the communicative constitution of organization (CCO) thinking and theorizing is a promising direction and 'home' for future research. This is a field of communication studies that:

> Can be analyzed either quantitatively or qualitatively, by focusing on narratives, interactions, texts, behaviors [sic] or even artifacts and architectural elements. What matters is that these studies remain grounded in action or, more precisely, in communication (as the central social practice), whether they get inspiration from network analysis, semiotics, conversation analysis, rhetoric or speech act theory, among many other possible approaches. (Cooren et al., 2011, pp. 1153–1154)

CCO thinking offers methodological fluidity and flexibility; and I contend that researchers seeking to future-proof their scholarship in the real-world(s) of both practice and academia will also need to have a degree of methodological curiosity and courage. Thirdly, the COVID-19 pandemic has triggered a global recession; its ultimate impact on economic history and the social history of gossip is yet to be written. Unquestionably, the pandemic will continue to disrupt all communicative practices, organizations, workplaces, and spaces for the foreseeable future. Researchers and practitioners are currently facing a crucial issue:

What happens in the absence of gossip?

For example, does it lead to demotivation, automation, disruption to innovation, and a breakdown in the fabric of an organization? What new forms/variants of gossip are emerging and evolving? Are there any unexpected positive outcomes? These are significant questions representing an important and immediate priority for research at this unique moment in the history of business and management research. They are also questions that can be answered using mixed methods and qualitative research.

Mixed methods research

According to Tashakkori et al. (2021, p. 3, original emphasis), mixed methods research can be defined variously, in terms that include the 'third methodological movement … the third path [and] the *third research community*'. The underlying philosophical paradigm of pragmatism eschews concepts such as 'truth' and 'reality', focusing instead on 'what works', as the truth underpinning answers to research questions under investigation. Pragmatism rejects either/or choices associated with qualitative/quantitative paradigms and acknowledges that researchers' values play a large role in the interpretation of results. Cameron and Molina-Azorin (2011, p. 268) argued that 'mixed methods is here to stay [and] will become increasingly used by business and management researchers especially those continually trying to innovate'. Innovative use of mixed methods holds great potential and promise for researchers who are open to including arts-based practices such as literary writing, music, visual art, photography, or other media during any/all phases of the research process (Leavy, 2020).

The strength of mixed methods research lies in the *integration* of different methods and approaches within a study. This creates the potential to see things that have not yet been seen, giving access to insights and understanding that go *beyond* those provided by the use of qualitative and quantitative methods alone. Research questions guide investigations and are concerned with *unknown* aspects of a phenomenon of interest. Mixed methods designs can be: (i) concurrent, characterized by the collection of both types of data during the same stage of data collection; or (ii) sequential, with either qualitative or quantitative data collected in an initial stage, followed by another stage collecting the other type of data. This research lens focuses on the relationships within and among scholars doing research in the social and behavioural sciences. It is thus well suited to researchers wishing to maintain a focus on the behavioural aspects of the 'gossip triad', and the role of gossip in and between groups. For example, sequential studies could integrate sociometric data regarding gossip and social networks (Ellwardt, 2019) with in-depth qualitative interviews exploring contextual detail and relational dynamics. Mixed methods research can also be incorporated into case study designs, which involve investigation of real-life cases to capture complexity and detail.

Case study research is not bound to particular methods and has a tradition of gathering both qualitative and quantitative data as a way of generating holistic and in-depth knowledge using multiple sources of evidence (Stake, 2005; Yin, 2018). Identification of the 'case' is crucial, and could, for example, involve:

- A 'bounded system' defined in terms of time and place; e.g., an event, an activity, individuals, or groups.
- A contemporary phenomenon in a real-life context.

The COVID-19 pandemic is an obvious example of a contemporary phenomenon in a real-life context that is ripe for further research. For instance, mixed methods research could integrate survey data exploring motives to the gossip (Beersma & Van Kleef, 2012) in hybrid work environments, with qualitative analysis of the emotional content of virtual 'e-gossip' in digital and visual media. While the virus disrupted the opportunities, physical spaces, and places for face-to-face gossip, a positive outcome has been the rise in 'pandemic poetry'. This has arisen as people around the world have witnessed loss, experienced suffering and grief, and sought words of wisdom and hope. This is an unexpected gift for researchers and scholars who seek to incorporate poetic traditions into their work.

The fourth space

A significant signpost for future research is the notion of a *fourth space*: 'where the quantitative, qualitative, mixed methods, and poetic research traditions intersect to enable different and deeper levels of meaning making to occur' (Archibald & Onwuegbuzie, 2020, p. 153). This is a space where conventional methodologies created for problems of previous centuries may need to be rejected or repurposed. This is not to say that findings, insights, and theories arising from quantitative methodologies are redundant, far from it. They can be used as a springboard for future mixed methods and qualitative research into gossip that explores the 'narratives behind the numbers'. For example, developing fresh insights into trust and reputation in markets (Diekmann & Przepiorka, 2019); online reputation in the gig economy (Snijders & Matzat, 2019); or wider issues surrounding gossip and power inequalities (Farley, 2019). However, there are qualities of qualitative research that are now being called into question.

Post-qualitative inquiry: potential future direction, or wrong turn?

Current challenges for qualitative inquiry include new forms of data and empirical materials such as virtual and digital data. This calls into question 'traditional' data collected using interviews for example, and their relevance for understanding current life worlds (Flick, 2019). While Harley and Cornelisson (2020) urge qualitative researchers to conduct research that leads to rigorously derived theoretical insights without recourse to standardized procedures and protocols for data analysis. Standardized approaches and 'formulaic research' can also limit creativity in qualitative research (Alvesson & Gabriel, 2013; Cassell et al., 2018b). Future research might usefully include post-qualitative inquiry, which some see as an innovative methodology that deconstructs conventional qualitative methods such as coding (Thomas & Bellingham, 2021); but which others see as not a methodology at all (St Pierre, 2021).

Rather than getting tangled up in methodological, epistemological, and ontological knots, the important point is to recognize that post-qualitative inquiry is also an evolving area of research and scholarship. It may lead to new avenues and research agendas, or it may be a wrong turning. Without further research, it is too early to tell. Tracy (2020) advocates that we listen and learn from post-qualitative conversations, but continue to use qualitative methods and practices as tools for creating meaning and sensemaking. I agree, and would add *look and listen with an open mind*, in order to craft an innovative interdisciplinary research agenda.

Crafting an innovative interdisciplinary research agenda

While isolated studies, such as my own, have a place in the literature in the form of research monographs (Waddington, 2012), they cannot provide the depth and breadth of understanding that is possible with programmatic interdisciplinary research. Benoit and Holbert (2008, p. 615) argue that programmatic research, 'which systematically investigates an aspect of communication [viz. gossip] with a series of related studies across contexts or with multiple methods' is particularly valuable. Giardini and Wittek (2019) have sketched the contours of an emerging research programme based on the conceptual foundations, antecedents, dynamics, and consequences of gossip and reputation. They position gossip as a multifaceted phenomenon with the following features: (i) it is relational and triadic; (ii) morally laden; (iii) multifunctional; (iv) context dependent; and (v) has an evolutionary base. While Michelson et al. (2010, p. 371) note:

> The characteristics and features of gossip lend itself to a process-oriented approach whereby the beginning and, particularly, end points of gossip are not always easily identified. Gossip about a subject or person can temporarily disappear only for it to resurface at some later stage.

The features of gossip outlined above suggest that interdisciplinary frameworks of evidence and imaginative theorizing are required to further our understanding. Carefully crafted research designs and innovative methodologies are needed, but this by no means is a new idea. Daft (1983, p. 539, emphasis added) proposed that scholarly research is:

> A craft and that significant research outcomes are associated with the mastery of craft elements in the research process [which include] error and surprise, storytelling, *research poetry*, nonlinear decision making, common sense, firsthand knowledge, and research colleagues.

Research poetry

While the idea of research poetry may seem strange to a business research audience, it has, I suggest, an important place in the future scholarship of gossip as an evolving area of research. This is quite simply because methodological innovations typically develop as research paradigms shift and new research practices emerge. They emerge from what Leavy (2020, p. 86) refers to as a 'methods gap', observing that poetry has developed as an alternative to traditional research narratives and notions of a 'gap'. The field of research poetry now has a well-developed body of work, addressing both methodological and ethical issues (Faulkner, 2016, 2018). Further discussion has occurred around what constitutes (and differentiates) quality and '*good enough* research poetry' (Lahman et al., 2018, p. 1, original emphasis). Poetry is a form that draws attention to silence, space, and shifting perspectives. For instance, the following poem by Czech poet and

immunologist Miroslav Holub (1923–1998) explores what might lie behind
a mysterious closed door:

'The door'

Go and open the door.
    Maybe outside there's
    a tree, or a wood,
    a garden,
    or a magic city.

Go and open the door.
    Maybe a dog's rummaging.
    Maybe you'll see a face,
or an eye,
or the picture
    of a picture.

Go and open the door.
    If there's a fog
    it will clear.

Go and open the door.
    Even if there's only
    the darkness ticking,
    even if there's only
    the hollow wind,
    even if
        nothing
            is there,
go and open the door.

At least
there'll be
a draught.

        Source: Translated by Ian Milner; in Holub, 2006;
        reproduced with permission.

Scientific training and experience as a doctor influenced Holub's poetry,
and his work illustrates landscapes where science and poetry meet on equal
terms. The concept of 'The door' is based on a dual metaphor of *both* that
which restricts us (conventional research paradigms and methods) *and* of

taking risks (having open-minded methodological curiosity). The poem also speaks to the concept and metaphor of research as a mystery story introduced in Chapter 2 (see Practice Point 2.1, p. 30), while the lines 'Maybe outside there's a tree, or a wood' reflect Easterby-Smith et al.'s (2021, p. 69) 'tree as a metaphor for the research process'. The roots of the tree represent research traditions that inform different disciplinary/philosophical positions and influences on research design. The trunk represents interlinked features of research design with regard to ontology, epistemology, methodology, and methods/techniques. The leaves represent the collection of data and analysis, in the way that leaves collect energy from sunlight. The fruit(s) of the tree represent research findings and outputs, which may be 'hard' (quantitative), 'soft' (qualitative), or 'hybrid' (mixed methods). Bringing Holub's poetry together with the tree as a metaphor for the research process can lead to creative thinking about the art and science of gossip.

Poetry and gossip

The pairing of poetry and gossip may also seem odd to a business research and practitioner audience, but there is a wider context at play here. As outlined in Chapters 1 and 2, gossip has a long history, from the Greek *Agora* to contemporary digital discourse and 'e-gossip'. Gossip has also historically played a key part in literature. For example, gossip and rumour feature in Jane Austen's (1775–1817) novels, especially *Pride and Prejudice*. Interestingly, when people *talk* about the details of their daily lives and work it is considered gossip. Yet when Austen *writes* about the gossipy detail of her characters' daily lives and work, it is considered a plot device and literature. Spacks (1985, p. 4) has argued that drawing attention to analogies between gossip and literature 'both focuses attention on gossip's positive aspects and illuminates the dynamics of real texts'. Here, I draw attention to analogies between gossip and poetry, and how this can be developed in regard to inclusion of arts-based research practice.

Bennett (2018, p. 1) quotes from a Robert Frost 1956 lecture that 'gossip exalts in poetry'. Bennett's analysis of gossip and American poetry shows how 20th-century poetries used gossip as a method to expand the formal and rhetorical possibilities of lyric to uncover histories of sexuality. Lyric poetry, like gossip, expresses emotion, and Bennett argues that lyric is 'self-reflexively concerned with the matters of privacy that are so crucial to gossip' (p. 2). Similarly, Schoeman's (1994, p. 82) philosophical analysis of gossip concludes that privacy is essential to understanding gossip because 'we need the domains of life [public–private] so demarcated in order to properly gossip'. Bennett concludes that a more rigorous consideration of poetry – as a neglected archive with which to think differently about gossip

– is needed. Using poetry as a research approach and method offers a novel approach with which to explore more nuanced understandings of the characteristics and meanings of gossip.

Poetry as method

Poetry as a research approach and method 'offers a form for the *evocative* presentation of data' (Leavy, 2020, p. 85, emphasis added). Poetry thus can generate evocative images, which, as discussed in Chapter 2, are critical to the development of imaginative theorizing. Poems use words, rhythm, and space to provoke and create sensory scenes and images, where meaning *emerges* from the careful constitution of both language and its absence. Seen this way, a poem can be understood as something that can evoke a snippet of human experience such as gossip. Poetry as method is a form of creative writing that can be used: (i) to explore data in new ways; and (ii) as a reflexive device to convey some of the messier aspects of research such as emotion (Faulkner, 2018).

Poetry as a reflexive practice

Reflexivity is the way we critically reflect upon, analyze, and understand positionality in the research process. Although it has its roots in qualitative inquiry, reflexivity is important for *all* research contexts, power structures, identities, and intersections. Despite the supposed neutrality of quantitative methods, Dean (2017, p. 7) argues they are equally likely to involve 'implicit and unevaluated assumptions, incomplete descriptions of empirical and theoretical methods', as well as self-interest, conflicts of interest, and political conflicts. There may be some reticence and/or resistance to reflexive practice by quantitative researchers, and scholars steeped in the '*epistemic imperialism of science*' (Mazur, 2021, p. 1, emphasis added). Reflecting on the enticement in Holub's poem to 'Go and open the door', another verse, written using my own words, and as an example of reflexive practice, might be:

> Maybe outside
>   lies a way of finding an intellectual balance
>   between methodological, theoretical, and epistemological struggles.

Smith (2020) points to the value of writing poetry as a reflexive practice in qualitative inquiry, to enable alternative knowing, and the capacity for arts-based research more broadly to disrupt the way we see, live, and understand ourselves and others. Some business and management scholars and researchers are clearly comfortable with using poetic research traditions and representations. For example, in the fields of strategy (MacLean & MacIntosh, 2015) and consumer culture (Tonner, 2019). 'Poetic' is a term referring to 'literary criticism that deals with the nature, forms, and laws of poetry, a study of poetry or aesthetics, the practice of writing poetry' (Weick, 2004, p. 666). But what do poetic representations look like to researchers who are not necessarily poets? Or who have limited interest and/or experience of engaging with and critiquing poetry?

Lahman et al. (2018, p. 1) introduce the innovative idea of 'poemish':

> Poemish representations may be said to be research representations characterized by features of poetry and an effort to blend the aesthetics of poetry and science of research into something which may be said to be poem-like, a resemblance of a poem, ish, or poemish.

In practical terms, what this entails is illustrated in Practice Point 3.1, a literary reflexive activity that is intended to help with the understanding of concrete words in poetry in an experimental way.

Practice Point 3.1

Poetry as reflexive practice

- *Challenge*: Chose an abstract idea such as gossip, compassion, happiness, frustration.
- *Concrete words*: Create a list of all the concrete words you can think of that illustrate the abstract idea you have chosen.
- *Senses*: Reread your list of concrete words: are all the sense represented? Add more words as needed.
- *Poemish*: Form the beginnings of a poem from this list.

Practice Point 3.1 is also pertinent to practitioners and leaders seeking to become critically reflexive practitioners, defined as: 'questioning what we, and others, might be taking for granted – what is being said and not said – and examining the impact this has or might have' (Cunliffe, 2016, p. 741). By way of another practice-based example, Box 3.1 is an extract from a poem written by one of my doctoral students, Jodie Das. Jodie is a practitioner, educator, and consultant working in the field of domestic violence and abuse prevention. She wrote the poem after a particularly difficult and emotionally charged meeting with practitioners working across multiple professional disciplines (e.g., social work, health, and education).

BOX 3.1 LIKE YOU

My meaning's sincere, I aim to provide,
I *so* want to fix all the things you confide.
The problem *I* have, is I'm vulnerable too,
I'm tired and I'm broken and hurting like you.

The pain that you feel, infused with my own,
Is heavy between us and hasn't a home.
I'll Ignore it, like you, it might go away,
After all, it's just 'work', at the end of the day.

So, forgive what I've mastered, a skilled attitude,
Like you, I'm defensive, dismissive and rude.
And gone are *my* dreams that were held at the start,
The hope that I'd keep both our interests at heart.

I wanted to help you, but who's helping me?!
Like you I have targets, and nothing for tea.*
Like you, I feel torn, and I don't have a voice,
My presents are empty, though the label says 'choice'.

I've boxed up compassion, and filed it away,
It can't write reports, so has nothing to say.
So next time you feel that my gestures are token,
Remember, like you, I've had promises broken.

*Tea is a British term sometimes used to denote the main evening
  meal.

Source: Extract from an unpublished personal/reflective poem
by Jodie Das, written on 30 April 2021, as part of a doctorate in
professional practice (DProf) health sciences at the University of
Westminster, UK; reproduced with permission.

Jodie's research aims to transform practice towards more equitable, ethical, and socially just outcomes when working preventatively with domestic violence and abuse (Das & Waddington, 2020). The poem 'Like you' vividly describes the tensions, frustrations, and deep emotions associated with her work. It also illustrates the power of poetry in expressing and managing emotion.

The chapter now shifts away from the realm of research poetry to that of critical participatory action research and organizational autoethnography. These are perhaps more familiar realms of research and are lenses that, I contend, are particularly pertinent to a real-world research agenda.

Critical participatory action research

Critical participatory action research is a collaborative commitment to engaging in iterative cycles of planning, acting, observing, and reflecting to address untoward consequences of social practice. Its aim is to change how people understand their practices, and the conditions/contexts in which they occur (Kemmis et al., 2014). Key features of this research lens are that practices are always reflexive and guided by ethical principles. Critical participatory action research is a particularly pertinent approach for future practice-/practitioner-based research that seeks to explore the 'sentinel' function of gossip as an early warning sign of future failure and scandal. Notably, Cunliffe (2016, pp. 740–741) comments that scandals 'are often linked to irresponsible decision making, poor workplace relationships, and [a] lack of reflexivity on the part of managers'. She argues that a *critically* reflexive approach involves examination and scrutiny of unintended ethical consequences of institutional policies and practices. A reflexive awareness of the *ethical consequences* of gossip as a communicative practice and process will be key to future research. Kemmis et al. (2014) use the term 'communicative action', understood as what happens when people feel there is 'something not quite right'. When people experience doubts and discomfort, and interrupt what they are doing to ask: 'What is going on here?' And if gossip is to be understood as an early warning sign of future failure and scandal, to ask again: 'But what is *really* going on here?' This crucial question repositions the phenomenon of gossip, away from the realm of trivial talk and degraded discourse, to something that is constitutive of organizational problems and risks to reputation. These issues and questions are explored further in Chapter 5, but now the chapter turns to address the potential value of the lens of organizational autoethnography.

Organizational autoethnography

Autoethnography has been described as 'the science of writing your lived experience' (O'Hara, 2018, p. 14). It is the systematic study, analysis, and narrative description of one's own culture, experiences, interactions, conversations, and identity; it also includes critical reflection, emotional recall, and systematic introspection (Tracy, 2020). Approaches range along a continuum from analytic, which limits the use of self to that of enhanced researcher reflexivity (Anderson, 2006), to evocative, emotional acts of subjective storytelling and sensemaking (Ellis & Bochner, 2006). As a systematic process, autoethnography involves:

(i) selecting an approach; (ii) ensuring ethical responsibility; (iii) deciding theoretical underpinnings; (iv) assembling and gathering data; (v) reflecting and analyzing; and (vi) disseminating work with supporting drawings, photography, and other evocative formats. Yet the question '*Is this research?*' has haunted autoethnography, which has been criticized for being self-indulgent, sentimental navel-gazing, non-scientific storytelling, too artful, and not artful enough (Denzin, 2014). Autoethnographers strongly refute these claims, arguing that they can be reinterpreted as productive tensions, and that embracing diverse perspectives strengthens the depth of engagement, quality, and potential impact. The goal is 'not to produce a standard social science article' (Denzin, 2014, p. 70); instead, the purpose of autoethnographic writing is to create *resonance*.

But what makes an autoethnography an *organizational* autoethnography? Hermann (2020) notes that organizational ethnographies use personal experiences to comment on discomforting and taboo topics, such as sexual harassment, bullying, racism, oppression, and moral dilemmas, in the workplace. Taboo derives from the Tongan *tabu* and the more general Polynesian term *tapu* meaning 'not allowed'. Arguably the erstwhile neglect of gossip in business research can be attributed to its perception as a taboo, or 'tainted research topic'. However, organizational autoethnography affords a research lens with which to amplify and imagine new understandings and give in-depth insights into gossip in the everyday world of work. This includes the everyday world of work in academia. Innovative forms used in recent academic authoethnographies into identity and identity work include vignettes (Fernando et al., 2020), and visual methods (Hunter, 2020). There is scope to extend these forms to organizational autoethnographies of gossip in the academia. This involves scholars of gossip, as reflective and reflexive practitioners, being recast as participant observers, listeners, and interpreters of gossip in and around their own institutions and disciplines.

Gossip in the academy

I can recall the *exact moment* in 1991 when I encountered a snippet of gossip that triggered my subsequent scholarly interest in gossip and organizations. I was conducting a qualitative interview for a small study into perceptions of university culture with a senior, and slightly cynical, humanities academic, whom I will call Bill (pseudonym). This was my first academic post, and having come from a clinical background working in hospital settings,

I was struck by the differences between healthcare and higher education cultures and wanted to know more. As an exemplar of arts-based autoethnographic research practice, in Box 3.2 I narrate this epiphany moment in the format of creative non-fiction (Sinner et al., 2018) and short story called 'Ah! Now I get it!'.

BOX 3.2 AH! NOW I GET IT!

It's the end of July 1991 in a hot empty classroom. I'm a bit nervous, this is my first research interview, and I find Bill [pseudonym] a bit scary. His area is humanities and English literature, not healthcare or psychology. *Help!!!* The dean helped to set up the interview, saying kindly, *he's been around a long time and has a lot to offer for your research.* I've practised with the tape recorder to make sure I press the right buttons so it records properly. I've practised my interview questions. I'm ready. Bill sits opposite me with a wry smile on his face. When I ask the question *Tell me, why are things done the way they are around here?* Bill says nothing. He gets up and moves his chair to an open window. I follow with my tape recorder, worried that the power cable might not reach. He stretches his legs out, rolls a cigarette, lights it, takes a long drag, and exhales smoke out of the open window. He points to the tape recorder, with the roll-up clamped between his first and second fingers: *Switch that off, Kathryn, and I'll tell you.* Bill then tells me 'high-octane gossip' about conflict and power struggles between departmental heads. It's 'off the record'. Oh well, I needn't have worried about the tape recorder. But what Bill has given me is more useful than a few lines in an interview transcript. I now know more about internal politics and turf wars. I now 'get' why it took so long to find office space for Jo [pseudonym for a colleague who started at the same time] and me. And why in our gossipy conversations in a shared office we say things like: *working here feels a bit like being in the Gulf War!* I think to myself ... *hmmm, there might be something more to this gossip malarkey** ...

* A phrase referring to 'meaningless talk' that came into use in the 1920s; origin unknown.

Source: A creative non-fiction short story (see Sinner et al., 2018).

The story in Box 3.2 reveals the anxieties of a novice researcher, and some subtle gendered power dynamics at play, but in a helpful, not harmful way.

Bill had useful knowledge to impart – as gossip – which helped me to navigate the unfamiliar political landscape and organizational culture I had ventured into. Yes, he might have been 'showing off' his 'superior male knowledge' to the 'new girl on the block'. Yes, this might even have been an early example of 'mansplaining' (Solnit, 2014). However, Bill's 'high-octane gossip' provided me with the 'fuel' to get me to where I am today in writing this book!

Reflecting on my 30 years' experience in higher education in a range of roles, including academic leadership, I have concluded that universities contain a 'rich seam' of gossip. I use the term 'rich seam' deliberately and metaphorically. In other words, as an underground layer of minerals – such as gold or coal – which may be precious and valuable (gold), or poisonous and harmful (coal, which, in a carbon-constrained climate, is poisoning the planet). This metaphor therefore reflects *both* the harmful aspects of gossip, for example as a form of bullying (Pheko, 2018), *and* its value, for example as a means of expressing and managing emotion (Martinescu et al., 2019). It also reflects the subterranean nature of gossip as 'knowledge underground' discussed earlier in the chapter.

A trend is emerging, illustrated by recent autoethnographic studies (see Table 3.1), which point to the rich seam of 'gossip in the academy' waiting to be mined in our universities.

The autoethnographic studies in Table 3.1 are written by academics working in Africa, Australia, and Europe. They illustrate both evocative (Liu & Pechenkina, 2019; van de Berg, 2021) and analytic (Pheko, 2018) autoethnography, and the value of thinking with theory. They all shed light on the 'dark side of university life' (Waddington, 2019, p. 243), the pressures of working in neoliberal institutions, and the dangerous culture of 'fast academia'. They all feature gossip to a greater or lesser degree, and they all point to the glimmerings of gossip as an early warning sign of underlying problems of bullying/hurtful cultures and organizational violence.

In the conclusion to *Gossip and Organizations*, I commented:

> I'm curious as to what the future might hold now that gossip has been brought into the foreground. What iterative insights might 'gossip about gossip' generate in academic and practitioner communities? Will current and future scholars of gossip be treated with suspicion as writers enmeshed in a morally contentious discourse? Or will we be seen as trustworthy colleagues with whom 'off the record' comments can be shared at conferences and in corridors? (Waddington, 2012, p. 160)

Table 3.1 Gossip in the academy

Author/title	Academic context	Methodological/theoretical aspects	Key findings/comments
Pheko (2018): Rumours and gossip as tools of social undermining and social dominance in workplace bullying and mobbing practices: a closer look at perpetrator motives	Case study of psychology lecturers/professors (3F; 1M) in a university in Botswana [established in 1982, and not a 'historically white university'] who self-identified as victims of bullying A 'non' WEIRD – White, Educated, Industrialized, Rich, Democratic – study	Collaborative analytic autoethnography; stories, emails, letters of complaint, reports, diaries, observations; grounded theory approach Social dominance theory; societies producing stable economic surplus organized as group-based social hierarchies of male power	Rumours and gossip as: (i) a tool for maintaining oppression/social dominance; (ii) expression of envy and social undermining; (iii) a weapon of humiliation; (iv) an attempt to widen the power gap Academic jealousy, competition, and fight for survival by the two *foreign professors*, because our *promotion as locals* would have [meant] that their contracts might not be renewed (p. 80, emphasis added)
Liu & Pechenkina (2019): Innovation-by-numbers: an autoethnography of innovation as violence	Australian Business School context and strategic priority of innovation capability and transformation of Australia's long-term prospects; disciplinary context of critical theory Concerns that trends towards blended/online learning mask reduction in contact hours/costs in a casualized academic workforce	Dual-perspective autoethnography presented as two creative non-fiction stories from: (i) the innovation/curriculum redesign workshop facilitator; (ii) a lecturer required to undertake innovation training Knowledge work and discourses of innovation; theorizing innovation as gendered and racialized organizational violence, expressed as shame, anxiety, anger	Innovation as: (i) 'symbolic capital' leading to struggles of control and compliance; (ii) exercise of managerial dominance; and (iii) autoethnographic writing as an act of resistance Rumour and gossip prevailed about 'difficult' academics who resisted the process of innovation (p. 180)

van de Berg (pseudonym) (2021): 'And we gossip about my life as if I am not there': An autoethnography on recovery from infidelity and silence in the academic workplace	Anonymized female Dutch psychologist narrating a story of shame, blame, and secrecy surrounding her husband's infidelity Problematic workplace culture of 'fast academia'	Thinking with theory to counter critique of autoethnography as voyeurism Feminist scholarship and intersectionality	(i) Toxic secrets, 'secret emotional life of academics'; (ii) hurtful silencing, 'denying feelings'; (iii) healing silence, 'sharing stories and non-intrusive acceptance by colleagues' Need for 'new, societally and academically relevant questions' (p. 15)

I remain curious about gossipy conversations in corridors and at conferences, but with a fresh curiosity about newly constituted spaces in the academy, where 'e-gossip' might emerge and evolve.

Autoethnography and conference conversations

Schmidt (2018) points to the similarities between gossip and poetry criticism, which:

> Opens up welcome space to think about critics themselves – or *perhaps reviewers* is the better word – as performing something akin to gossip in their writings and talks, trashing certain poets' [academics'] reputations, *lifting others into the fold.* (p. 397, emphasis added)

The above quote is, I suggest, synonymous with conference conversations, and academic peer-review processes and politics. Does it resonate with your experience of academic peer-review processes and conference conversations? Think back honestly to the last time you were at a face-to-face conference or professional gathering. Reflect on the public–private and formal–informal conversations and interactions. Do your thoughts and reflections resonate with these of a research participant in a qualitative study into the role of gossip in nursing and healthcare organizations:

> I think the most *interesting* part of going to a conference is what goes on outside the lecture hall, and *we all know* that's where the *real work* gets done, and that's also *where the gossip takes place.* [So] there's nothing like a few glasses of wine for people to start to talk … and it could be harmless, or poisonous [male clinical academic]. (Waddington, 2012, p. 47, emphasis added)

This interview extract illustrates the relationship between gossip and reputation, which are multifaceted phenomena and core processes in all human societies (Giardini & Wittek, 2019). The extract can also be interpreted as 'knowledge in the making', which strikes a chord with the conceptual thread of gossip as a pathway to knowledge that is woven throughout the book. As Gross and Fleming (2011, p. 152) note, 'keeping up with the latest academic gossip [and other activities] … suggests that conferences can be key sites for the orchestration of academic knowledge'. This was certainly the case pre-pandemic, but what of the future? Gossip is a core human and evolutionary process, and rather than being annihilated by the virus, when seen as a communicative practice and constitutive organizational process, gossip will simply adapt and evolve. This is for future researchers to experience and explore, and arguably something that makes gossip, as an evolving area of scholarship and research in this series, all the more exciting, and also, all the more challenging.

Challenges and pragmatic solutions

This chapter has laid out an ambitious research agenda for researching real-world lived experiences of gossip, bringing together a range of approaches and adding arts-based methods and practices into the mix. This raises challenges for journal editors and reviewers who are antithetical towards qualitative (let alone arts-based) research, and/or 'are not capable or competent to review writing in this genre' (Denzin, 2018, p. 676). Debates continue to rage, including the status and quality of qualitative business and management research, and the inappropriate use of homogenous evaluation criteria (Cassell et al., 2018b).

There are also challenges facing researchers who choose to use methods and practices that run counter to the more conventional and powerful paradigms in business and management research. This is particularly the case for early career researchers, who occupy precarious positions in competitive environments, staking out their disciplinary identities, reputations, and track records of research in prestigious journals. Denzin (2018) argues that the mainstream resistances to critical qualitative inquiry cannot be overcome, and that 'multiple mainstreams' (p. 676) are required; therefore, new boats are needed. To paraphrase Audre Lorde (1984) – and substituting boats for houses – it is not possible to use the boat maker's tools to dismantle his [sic] boat. We need to build different boats using new research tools and create 'general and evolving criteria for evaluation' (Leavy, 2018, p. 575) that can be applied appropriately, judiciously, and pragmatically.

Some pragmatic solutions

For Leavy (2018) the main point is that it is possible to have general criteria, as well as genre- and practice-specific criteria, or what Faulkner (2016, p. 662) terms 'flexible criteria'. There are numerous general evaluation criteria and critical appraisal tools for quantitative, qualitative, and mixed methods research, which are not repeated in detail here; but see, for example, the Canadian Mixed Methods Appraisal Tool (MMAT, 2018). Leavy (2018, pp. 577–578) suggests the following overarching criteria for evaluating studies using/integrating arts-based methods:

- *Methodology*: how the research was carried out and the rationale/justification.
- *Usefulness and significance*: the substantive/practical contribution.
- *Public scholarship*: accessibility to diverse audiences inside/outside academia.
- *Response to research*: the effect upon those who read and use the research.
- *Creativity and curiosity*: the unique quality the researcher brings to their work.
- *Ethics*: attention to values and moral judgements guiding research decisions.

The above overarching criteria for evaluation can then be incorporated, *as appropriate*, alongside more familiar evaluation criteria. A reminder: an arts-based approach can be used *in any or all of the stages of the research process*. It may be wise to start small, for instance, in identifying the research topic and/or disseminating findings. Or consider using music, art, literature, poetry, film, and so forth as a reflexive device – no matter what your methodological preference/position – to consider the following question:

> *How am I taking into account my assumptions, values, feelings, and decisions throughout the research process?*

Concluding reflections

I hope this chapter has added some new thinking to the scholarly 'tool bag' of methods and approaches to business and management research. I use the metaphor of a 'tool bag' – rather than a 'fixed' tool shed – because researchers will need to be flexible rather than fixed in their approach. Some of the more traditional 'tried and tested' methods and tools now need to be left at home. In my 'home' discipline of psychology, Mazur (2021) argues that there has been an almost neurotic obsession to be seen as scientific; and the subjective world, rather like a null hypothesis, has been rejected. He asserts that it is time to return to the notion of *sapientia*, a Latin term meaning 'wisdom', which, like gossip, escapes clear, fixed definition. 'Like the haiku,[1] [sapientia] breaks free of representation, be it in numbers, words, linearity, circularity, and sequentiality' (Mazur, 2021, p. 6). This critique of positivism extends beyond psychology and the social sciences to business and management disciplines, where the tendency towards positivist/postpositivist reductionism and quantification has distracted attention away from ordinary, everyday phenomena such as gossip. This is not to say that science and quantitative research do not have a place in the future, far from it. They just may not occupy such a dominant place. I conclude with a quote by the exiled social scientist Gustav Ichheiser (1897–1969) – as cited in Mazur (2021, p. 10) – which I hope will find some resonance for readers and future researchers:

> We should not expect and demand that everything should be 'proved.' To say it once more, social scientists should, in my opinion, not aspire to be as 'scientific' and 'exact' as physicists or mathematicians, but should *cheerfully* accept the fact that what they are doing belongs to the twilight zone between science and literature.

Note

1 The haiku is an unrhymed Japanese poem traditionally arranged in three lines, often used as a celebration of nature, but its traditional rules can also be broken.

References

Allen, M. (Ed.) (2017). *The SAGE encyclopedia of organizational communication research methods*. Thousand Oaks, CA: SAGE Publications.

Alvesson, M., & Gabriel, Y. (2013). Beyond formulaic research: In praise of greater diversity in organizational research and publications. *Academy of Management Learning & Education, 12*(2), 245–263. doi: 10.5465/amle.2012.0327

Alvesson, M., & Sköldberg, K. (2018). *Reflexive methodology: New vistas for qualitative research*. London: SAGE Publications.

Anderson, L. (2006). Analytic autoethnography. *Journal of Contemporary Ethnography, 35*(4), 373–395. doi: 10.1177/0891241605280449

Archibald, M. M., & Onwuegbuzie, A. J. (2020). Poetry and mixed methods research. *International Journal of Multiple Research Approaches*, 12(2), 153–165. doi: 10.29034/ijmra.v12n2editorial3

Arnold, J., Dries, N., & Gabriel, Y. (2021). EJWOP special issue: Enhancing the social impact of research in work and organizational – Beyond academia. *European Journal of Work and Organizational Psychology, 30*(3), 329–338. doi: 10.1080/1359432X.2021.1915293

Bazeley, P. (2019). *A practical introduction to mixed methods for business and management*. London: SAGE Publications.

Beersma, B., & Van Kleef, G. A. (2012). Why people gossip: An empirical analysis of social motives, antecedents, and consequences. *Journal of Applied Psychology, 42*(11), 2640–2670. doi: 10.1111/j.1559-1816.2012.00956.x

Bennett, C. (2018). *Word of mouth: Gossip and American poetry*. Baltimore, MD: Johns Hopkins University Press.

Benoit, W. L., & Holbert, R. L. (2008). Empirical intersections in communication research: Replication, multiple quantitative methods, and bridging the quantitative–qualitative divide. *Journal of Communication, 58*, 615–628. doi: 10.1111/j.1460-2466.2008.00404.x

Breslin, D. (2021). Darwin, evolution, and compassion in the 21st-century university. In K. Waddington (Ed.), *Towards the compassionate university: From golden thread to global impact* (pp. 39–52). Abingdon: Routledge.

Cameron, R., & Molina-Azorin, J. F. (2011). The acceptance of mixed methods in business and management research. *International Journal of Organizational Analysis, 19*(3), 256–271. doi: 10.1108/19348831111149204

Cassell, C., Cunliffe, A. L., & Grandy, G. (Eds.) (2018a). *The SAGE handbook of qualitative business and management research methods.* London: SAGE Publications.

Cassell, C., Cunliffe, A. L., & Grandy, G. (2018b). Introduction: Qualitative research in business and management. In C. Cassell, A. L. Cunliffe, & G. Grandy (Eds.), *The SAGE handbook of qualitative business and management research methods* (pp. 1–14). London: SAGE Publications.

Cooren, F., Kuhn. T., Cornelissen, J. P., & Clark, T. (2011). Communication, organizing and organizing: An overview and introduction to the special issue. *Organization Studies, 32*(9), 1149–1170. doi: 10.1177/0170840611410836

Cunliffe, A. L. (2016). 'On becoming a critically reflexive practitioner' redux: What does it mean to *be* reflexive? *Journal of Management Education, 40*(6), 740–746. doi: 10.1177/1052562916668919

Daft, R. L. (1983). Learning the craft of organizational research. *Academy of Management Review, 8*(4), 539–546. doi: 10.5465/amr.1983.4284649

Das, J., & Waddington, K. (2020). Building better relationships: Developing critically reflective practice when working preventively with domestic violence and abuse. *International Practice Development Journal, 10*(2), 1–9. doi: 10.19043/ipdj.102.012.

Dean, J. (2017). *Doing reflexivity: An introduction.* Bristol: Policy Press.

Denzin, N. K. (2014). *Interpretive ethnography* (2nd ed.) Thousand Oaks, CA: SAGE Publications.

Denzin, N. K. (2018). The pragmatics of publishing experimental text. In P. Leavy (Ed.), *Handbook of arts-based research* (pp. 673–688). New York: The Guildford Press.

Diekmann, A., & Przepiorka, W. (2019). Trust and reputation in markets. In F. Giardini, & R. Wittek (Eds.), *The Oxford handbook of gossip and reputation* (pp. 383–400). New York: Oxford University Press.

Easterby-Smith, M., Jaspersen, L. J., Thorpe, R., & Valizade, D. (Eds). (2021). *Management and business research* (7th ed.) London: SAGE Publications.

Ellis, C. S., & Bochner, A. P. (2006). Analyzing analytic autoethnography: An autopsy. *Journal of Contemporary Ethnography, 35*(4), 429–449. doi: 10.1177/0891241606286979

Ellwardt, L. (2019). Gossip and reputation in social networks. In F. Giardini, & R. Wittek (Eds.), *The Oxford handbook of gossip and reputation* (pp. 435–457). New York: Oxford University Press.

Eriksson, P., & Kovalainen, A. (Eds). (2016) *Qualitative methods in business research* (2nd ed.) London: SAGE Publications.

Farley, S. (2019). On the nature of gossip, reputation, and power inequality. In F. Giardini, & R. Wittek (Eds.), *The Oxford handbook of gossip and reputation* (pp. 343–358). New York: Oxford University Press.

Faulkner, S. L. (2016). The art of criteria: *Arts criteria* as demonstration of vigor in poetic inquiry. *Qualitative Inquiry, 22*(8), 662–665. doi: 10.1177/1077800416634739

Faulkner, S. L. (2018). Poetic inquiry. In P. Leavy (Ed.), *Handbook of arts-based research* (pp. 208–230). New York: The Guildford Press.

Fernando, M., Reveley, J., & Learmonth, M. (2020). Identity work by a non-white immigrant business scholar: Autoethnographic vignettes of covering and accenting. *Human Relations, 73*(6), 765–788. doi: 10.1177/0018726719831070

Flick, U. (2019). The concepts of qualitative data: Challenges in neoliberal times for qualitative inquiry. *Qualitative Inquiry, 25*(8), 713–720. doi: 10.1177/1077800418809132

Giardini, F., & Wittek, R. (2019). Introduction: Gossip and reputation – A multidisciplinary research program. In F. Giardini, & R. Wittek (Eds.), *The Oxford handbook of gossip and reputation* (pp. 1–20). New York: Oxford University Press.

Gross, N., & Fleming, C. (2011). Academic conferences and the making of philosophical knowledge. In C. Camic, N. Gross, & Lamont, M. (Eds.), *Social knowledge in the making* (pp. 151–180). Chicago, IL: University of Chicago Press.

Harley, B., & Cornelisson, J. (2020). Rigor without templates? The pursuit of methodological rigor in qualitative research. *Organizational Research Methods* [online]. Available at: 10.1177/1094428120937786 [Accessed 1 July 2021].

Hermann, A. F. (2020). The historical and hysterical narratives of organization and autoethnography. In A. Hermann (Ed.), *The Routledge international handbook of autoethnography* (pp. 13–40). Abingdon: Routledge.

Holub, M. (2006, translated by Ian Milner). *Poems before and after*. Hexham: Bloodaxe Books Ltd.

Hunter, A. (2020). Snapshots of selfhood: Curating academic identity through visual autoethnography. *International Journal for Academic Development, 25*(4), 310–323. doi: 10.1080/1360144X.2020.1755865

Kemmis, S., McTaggart, R., & Nixon, R. (2014). A new view of practices: Practices held in place by practice architectures. In S. Kemmis, R. McTaggart, & R. Nixon (Eds.), *The action research planner: Doing critical participatory action research* (pp. 51–66). Cham: Springer.

Lahman, M., Teman, E., & Richard, V. (2018). ish: How to write poemish (research) poetry. *Qualitative Inquiry, 25*(2), 215–227. doi: 10.1177/1077800417750182

Leavy, P. (2018). Criteria for evaluating arts-based research. In P. Leavy (Ed.), *Handbook of arts-based research* (pp. 575–586). New York: The Guildford Press.

Leavy, P. (2020). *Method meets art: Arts-based research practice*. New York: The Guildford Press.

Liu, H., & Pechenkina, E. (2019). Innovation-by-numbers: An autoethnography of innovation as violence. *Culture and Organization, 25*(3), 178–188. doi: 10.1080/14759551.2017.1361422

Lorde, A. (1984). *Sister outsider: Essays and speech*. Trumansburg, NY: Crossing Press.

MacLean, D., & MacIntosh, R. (2015). Planning reconsidered: Paradox, poetry and people at the edge of strategy. *European Management Journal, 33*(2), 72–78. doi: 10.1016/j.emj.2015.02.003

Martinescu, E., Jannsen, O., & Nijstad, B. A. (2019). Gossip and emotion. In F. Giardini, & R. Wittek (Eds.), *The Oxford handbook of gossip and reputation* (pp. 152–169). New York: Oxford University Press.

Mazur, L. B. (2021). The epistemic imperialism of science. Reinvigorating early critiques of scientism. *Frontiers in Psychology* [online]. Available at: 10.3389/fpsyg.2020.609823 [Accessed 15 July 2021].

Michelson, G., van Iterson, A., & Waddington, K. (2010). Gossip in organizations: Contexts, consequences, and controversies. *Group & Organization Management, 35*(4), 371–390. doi: 10.1177/1059601109360389

MMAT (2018). Mixed methods appraisal tool: User guide [online]. Available at: http://mixedmethodsappraisaltoolpublic.pbworks.com/w/file/fetch/127916259/MMAT_2018_criteria-manual_2018-08-01_ENG.pdf [Accessed 1 July 2021].

O'Hara, S. (2018). Autoethnography: The science of writing your lived experience. *Health Environments Research & Design Journal, 11*(4), 14–17. doi: 10.1177/1937586718801425

Pheko, M. M. (2018). Rumors and gossip as tools of social undermining and social dominance in workplace bullying and mobbing practices: A closer look at perceived perpetrator motives. *Journal of Human Behavior in the Social Environment, 28*(4), 449–465. doi: 10.1080/10911359.2017.1421111

Pietroni, P. (2019). *The poetry of compassion.* Albuquerque, NM: Fresco Books.

Putnam, L. L., & Mumby, D. K. (Eds.) (2014). *The SAGE handbook of organizational communication: Advances in theory, research and methods* (3rd ed.) Thousand Oaks, CA: SAGE Publications.

Schmidt, C. (2018). Dishing dirt in poetry's house of fame. *Contemporary Literature, 38*(3), 397–403.

Schoeman, F. (1994). Gossip and privacy. In R. F. Goodman, & A. Ben-Ze'ev (Eds.), *Good gossip* (pp. 72–84). Kansas, KS: University of Kansas.

Sinner, A., Hasebe-Ludt, E., & Leggo, C. (2018). Long story short: Encounters with creative nonfiction as methodological provocation. In P. Leavy (Ed.), *Handbook of arts-based research* (pp. 165–189). New York: The Guildford Press.

Smith, E. B. (2020). Poetry as reflexivity: (Post) reflexive poetic composition. *Qualitative Inquiry, 26*(7), 875–877. doi: 10.1177/1077800419879202

Snijders, C., & Matzat, U. (2019). Online reputation systems. In F. Giardini, & R. Wittek (Eds.), *The Oxford handbook of gossip and reputation* (pp. 479–495). New York: Oxford University Press.

Solnit, R. (2014). *Men explain things to me.* London: Granta.

Spacks, P. M. (1985). *Gossip.* New York, NY: Alfred A. Knopf.

St Pierre, E. A. (2021). Post qualitative inquiry, the refusal of method, and the risk of the new. *Qualitative Inquiry, 27*(1), 3–9. doi: 10.1177/10778004419863005

Stake, R. E. (2005). *Multiple case study analysis.* New York: The Guildford Press.

Tashakkori, A. M., Johnson, R. B., & Teddlie, C. (2021). *Foundations of mixed methods research: Integrating quantitative and qualitative approaches in the social and behavioural sciences* (2nd ed.) Thousand Oaks, CA: SAGE Publications.

Thomas, M. K. E., & Bellingham, R. (Eds.) (2021). *Post-qualitative research and innovative methodologies.* London: Bloomsbury Academic.

Tonner, A. (2019). Consumer culture poetry: Insightful data and methodological approaches. *Consumption Markets & Culture,* *22*(3), 256–271. doi: 10.1080/10253866.2018.1474110

Tracy, S. J. (2020). *Qualitative research methods: Collecting evidence, crafting analysis, communicating impact* (2nd ed.) Hoboken, NJ: John Wiley & Sons.

van de Berg, T. (pseudonym). (2021). And we gossip about my life as if I am not there: An autoethnography on recovery from infidelity and silence in the academic workplace. *Human Relations* [online]. Available at: 10.1177/00187267211022264 [Accessed 1 July 2021].

Waddington, K. (Ed.) (2021). *Towards the compassionate university: From golden thread to global impact.* Abingdon: Routledge.

Waddington, K. (2012). *Gossip and organization.* Abingdon: Routledge.

Waddington, K. (2019). Understanding and creating compassionate institutional cultures and practices. In P. Gibbs, J. Jameson, & A. Elwick (Eds.), *Values of the university in a time of uncertainty* (pp. 241–259). Cham: Springer.

Weick, K. E. (2004). Mundane poetics: Searching for wisdom in organization studies. *Organization Studies, 5*(4), 653–668. doi: 10.1177/0170840604042408

Wodak, R., & Meyer, M. (Eds.) (2016). *Methods of critical discourse analysis* (3rd ed.) London: SAGE Publications.

Yin, R. K. (2018). *Case study research and applications* (6th ed.) Thousand Oaks, CA: SAGE Publications.

4 Researching organizational gossip

Ethical considerations

Gossip and ethics

There are three reasons for including the ethical considerations of researching gossip in the workplace as a chapter in its own right. Firstly, as I argued in Chapter 2, because organizational gossip can be situated in the field of applied social epistemology (Adkins, 2017; Bartolutti & Magnani, 2019; Coady & Chase, 2019). This is a field that straddles the boundary between epistemology and ethics, with a concern for relevance to the ordinary affairs of everyday life. Secondly, because there is *always* an evaluative component to gossip, which in some instances may occur as a response to perceived unfairness and/or social injustice (Boehm, 2019), reflecting a moral/ethical element. Thirdly, to offer further guidance regarding the ethical principles of researching gossip that relate to access, participation, consent, privacy, and confidentiality. The broad aim of this chapter therefore is: to enable researchers to demonstrate to participants, research users, and readers, funders, ethics committees, and other monitoring/review bodies that their organizational gossip research is: (i) ethically rigorous, relational, and reflexive; and (ii) culturally responsive.

Gossip can be seen as an example of 'everyday ethics in practice'; because as Clegg and van Iterson (2009, p. 279) note, it refers to 'what it is that people do and how they account for its doing in their everyday work and discourse'. They go on, however, to argue that this is not a 'positive' ethics, but rather an ethics of transgression and attempt to exercise 'power over', rather than an attempt to create ethical vitality. Thus there is something of a 'double-edged sword' here related to gossip valence – as positive vs. negative, malicious vs. non-malicious (see Tassiello et al., 2018). A core argument in this chapter is that gossip and ethics cannot be uncoupled; nor can they be constrained by narrow definitions and standardized ethical procedures. While standardized ethical procedures have some advantages, such as identifying explicit criteria and procedures for research, they also have

DOI: 10.4324/9780367652982-4

limitations that can lead to a tick box mentality. Inflexible implementation of standardized, overly bureaucratic ethical procedures has led to debates around 'ethics police' and 'ethical imperialism' (Stahl et al., p. 9). Similarly, while definitions have a role in directing research, 'they should not be used to brutally rule out communicative practices that are felt to be gossip even if they do not fall clearly within a given definition' (Bartolutti & Magnani, 2019, p. 273). As I argued in Chapter 2, attempts to police the field of gossip through definition are fairly futile, and it is preferable to think about gossip as an aspect of 'language in action' (Gabriel, 2018, p. 64). Gossip as a communicative practice of language in action is now breaking free from narrow definitions that can debilitate the development of new knowledge and thinking, but which needs sound ethical practice. The focus of this chapter reflects concurrent trajectories in the field of research ethics:

> Namely the increasingly explicit and formalised requirements of research governance and the ongoing debate around the implicit nature of ethics, which cannot be assured by these methods, and related – for some – the role that reflexivity can play in research ethics. (Jeanes, 2017, p. 174)

The chapter begins with a necessarily brief outline of key moral and ethical principles surrounding gossip as discourse. This is followed by consideration of ethical principles and practices for researching gossip in the workplace, including the challenges of maintaining confidentiality and anonymity. It concludes with recommendations for relational and reflexive ethics, and culturally responsive research.

Moral and ethical principles surrounding gossip as discourse

Gossip is evaluative talk, which in some instances will reflect a moral/ethical element of right or wrong. Westacott (2012, p. 99), writing from a normative ethics philosophical standpoint, argues that 'there is nothing *necessarily* wrong with gossip'. Normative ethics offers moral judgements on people and their behaviour in terms such as right, wrong, good, bad, acceptable, inexcusable, and so on. According to Westacott, gossip can be wrong, and subject to censorship for a number of reasons related to overarching moral principles when/if it:

- Contains malicious or self-serving lies.
- Violates someone's rights.
- Promotes more harm than good.

- Is disrespectful.
- Causes harm, for example to reputation, self-esteem/-confidence.

Westacott's argument for the censorship of gossip is based on utilitarianism, an ethical theory that determines right from wrong by focusing on outcomes; a form of consequentialism – the general doctrine in ethics that actions should be evaluated on the basis of their consequences (Hasnas, 2013). In regard to decision-making, it also holds that the most ethical choice is the one that will produce the greatest good for the greatest number. Utilitarianism stems from the late 18th- and 19th-century English philosophers and economists Jeremy Bentham and John Stuart Mill, according to whom an action (or type of action) is wrong if it produces unhappiness or pain, and right if it tends to produce happiness or pleasure (Duignan, n.d.). Ben-Ze'ev's (1994, p. 13) 'vindication of gossip' points to its fundamental features as a relaxing, easy-going, and enjoyable activity; but also, as something which enables people to talk about what is 'really on their mind'. In other words, something they are perhaps concerned and care about, which leads to further consideration of organizational gossip through the lens of an ethic of care.

Gossip and an ethic of care

By including, and integrating, an ethic of care (Gilligan, 1982/2009) to the ethical position outlined above, it becomes evident that harm may also arise as a consequence of *not attending* to gossip. In other words, when organizational gossip represents an expression of care and concern. This is the 'sentinel' feature of gossip; acting as an early warning of future failure and harm to individuals and institutions, but later revealed in analyses of retrospective public inquiries and investigations (see Chapter 1). Carol Gilligan's *In a Different Voice* is a foundational feminist text that established an ethic of care as the central value around which moral theory and practice might revolve. This is not to stereotype or position gossip as exclusively feminist discourse. Studies have shown how cattle ranchers in California used 'truthful negative gossip' (Kniffin & Wilson, 2010, p. 160) to resolve disputes informally. While Kniffin and Wilson's (2005) mixed methods ethnographic case study of a competitive men's rowing team in a US university showed how gossip was used to enforce group norms around expectations of teamwork, and to manage the behaviour of a 'free-rider'. It is also an excellent example of ethically rigorous real-world research.

Inclusion of a feminist ethic of care, as with inclusion of other aspects of feminist theory, research, and practice, may not 'sit' so easily and prominently within the field of critical management studies (CMS), despite the field's distinguishing concern surrounding the dynamics and exercise of power. Importantly, however, Bell et al. (2016, p. 57) suggest that an ethic of care may be seen as a complement to the ethic of justice 'which has traditionally formed the *raison d'être* for CMS'. They conclude that an ethic of care enables scholars to engage in the process of constituting a more diverse notion of academic subjectivity that more effectively includes marginalized groups. The starting point for an ethic of care is one where individuals are seen as being relational and interdependent, 'morally and epistemologically rather than independent, self-sufficient actors' (Lawrence & Maitlis, 2012, p. 641).

When is gossip ethically and morally acceptable?

Westacott (2012, p. 89) notes: '*Learning is enjoyable*: as Aristotle remarks, the desire to know is part of human nature'. This is an individualistic view, and other levels of analysis are also relevant to discussions about the nature of knowledge, and the role of gossip as a *pathway to knowledge* (Adkins, 2017; Ayim, 1994; Tooman et al., 2016). Key questions are: (i) *who* acquires, produces, and holds knowledge; and (ii) crucially, *why* and *how*? Knowledge at a group/collective level is more than the sum of individual members' information repositories. Collective knowledge 'constitutes shared meanings built upon the interaction of individuals and the development of organizational norms, systems and processes' (Tooman et al., 2016, p. 21). Mills's (2010) research, for example, illustrated how gossip was used to acquire knowledge about the personality and character of a new CEO. Ayim (1994, p. 95) argues that access to that knowledge gained 'via the grapevine' of 'large or important issues ... is of crucial importance [in] making decisions within the corporate world'. This is 'good gossip' (de Sousa, 1994; Goodman & Ben-Ze'ev, 1994; Westacott, 2012), with positive social and organizational consequences that can:

- Improve understanding of social/organizational reality.
- Facilitate the operation of social institutions.
- Counteract secrecy.
- Facilitate transparency.
- Help reinforce social mores.

Therefore, it is not so much *what* is being gossiped about that determines the positive consequences of gossip; rather it is the intent of the person(s) gossiping (De Backer et al., 2019). Nevertheless, the negative stereotypes and censorious attitudes that have surrounded gossip as ethically reprehensible, inauthentic discourse (Heidegger, 1962) have undoubtedly contributed to the minimal presence of gossip as a topic in business and organizational research. Notably, Heidegger's phenomenological account of language and view of gossip as 'superficial talk' misses a very important point, which is:

> The way in which gossip, particularly when done by those on the margins, is precisely *the work of struggle*. People whose *voices and views are routinely silenced or undermined* must be able to both navigate conventional viewpoints and understand the ways in which alternative viewpoints critique and undermine the conventional position. ... accounts of knowledge in relationship are incomplete as long as they don't recognise the ways in which *relationships all contain power dynamics*. [Heidegger's] account misses the way in which the work of philosophy in itself often fail to capture people's lived experience, and thus the ways in which a 'trivial' act like gossip can actually contain worthwhile content. (Adkins, 2017, pp. 32–33, emphasis added)

Thus, there is arguably more to be said in favour of gossip than against; gossip has unappreciated positive aspects worthy of further research, guided by appropriate and meaningful ethical principles, which are considered next.

Ethical principles for researching organizational gossip

This section draws upon the *Academy of Management Code of Ethics* (AOM, n.d.), the *American Psychological Association Ethical Principles* (APA, n.d.), and the *Australian Code for the Responsible Conduct of Research* (2018) to offer ethical principles for researching gossip. The term 'ethical principle' is used here in the manner advocated by Hasnas (2013, p. 280):

> I use the term "principle" in a highly inclusive way to refer to any form of normative guidepost, not to privilege a deontological approach to ethics. Thus, as I am using the term, ethical principles can refer to the guidance provided by any ethical theory, whether consequentialist, deontological, or virtue ethics in nature.

Ethical research principles involve taking into account issues and questions that go beyond narrow parameters of 'procedural ethics' such as approval from institutional review boards (IRBs) and research ethics committees (RECs). While such minimalist approaches are necessary to prevent harm to participants and researchers, and protect disciplinary, institutional and researcher reputations, they are inadequate on their own. Wider ethical issues and principles relate to the 'justification of human action' (Lahman et al., 2011, p. 1398) and the ways we constitute a legitimate and justified knowledge of social and organizational life. This includes paying attention to 'ethics in practice' within the research process in its *entirety* – from initial ideas for inquiry, research question/s and aims, choice of methodology and methods, reporting of findings in an honest and transparent manner, and publication(s). This extends beyond narrow 'procedural ethics' to include: (i) the concept of an ethical mindset (Issa & Pick, 2010); and (ii) awareness of 'ethically important moments' – the 'difficult, often subtle and usually unpredictable situations that arise in the practice of doing research' (Guillemin & Gillam, 2004, p. 262). Such ethical tensions are part of the everyday practice of doing research and extend to the reporting of research.

Ethical tensions

Tourish and Craig's (2020, p. 175) analysis of 131 articles retracted from peer-reviewed journals in business and management studies found:

> Tensions regarding ethical research practice are manifest in universities where performance management systems stress the importance of achieving high-profile outputs in prestigious journals. Such systems reward those who reach output targets and sanction those who do not.

While the tensions surrounding the practice(s) of academic publication in competitive, target-driven audit cultures are hardly unpredictable (e.g., see Bell et al., 2016), they are nonetheless ethically important. The point to be made here is that retraction of journal articles reflects unethical and deceptive research misconduct, which may well be known about and gossiped about by scholars and researchers in their respective fields. For example, in regard to misconduct in science, Vaidyanathan et al. (2016) interviewed 251 physicists and biologists from both elite and non-elite universities and research institutes in the US, UK, and India. They found that scientists are often reticent or unable to take formal action against behaviours they perceive as unethical and irresponsible, such as fabricating data. As a result, they resort to informal gossip to warn colleagues of transgressors. It is evident that gossip is a ubiquitous phenomenon, occurring in all societies, age groups, cultures, and communities, including scientific communities and research groups. This is illustrated in Box 4.3, a composite (i.e., based on more than one incident) creative non-fiction short story (Sinner et al., 2018), drawn from my experiences as an early career reflexive researcher of gossip, called 'So, I've just given you half an hour of data'.

BOX 4.1   SO, I'VE JUST GIVEN YOU HALF AN HOUR OF DATA

This comment was made following a gossipy conversation that took place on a train journey to a conference. Although it was said light-heartedly, there was also a sense of underlying indignation. I was travelling to the conference with Sam [pseudonym], an ex-colleague and friend. We were looking forward to catching up on the journey, having a gossip, as we hadn't seen each other for some time. When we got on the train, Sam said: 'Oh look, there's professor A. N. Other over there, let's go and sit with them'. I didn't know this professor, but it quickly became evident that they and Sam also had some catching up to do. I took a book out of my bag and started to read but was aware of the conversation going on around me. The talk moved on quickly from their respective conference papers to the relationships, research grants, publications, and promotions of people who were unknown to me. This was serious gossip, and not all of it was positive. I was in a dilemma. I felt simultaneously like an outsider, an intruder, an eavesdropper, and a voyeur. I sat quietly, trying to read my book, inwardly squirming. Eventually Sam turned to me and said: 'So go on, tell us about your paper,' and nodded towards their professorial colleague: 'Kathryn's interested in gossip at work, you know'. 'No, I didn't know', said Professor Other, rather acidly. There was a tangible silence, followed by: 'So, I've just given you half an hour of data' – there was a pause – 'for free'.

Source: A creative non-fiction short story (see Sinner et al., 2018).

Box 4.1 illustrates some of the ethical tensions I experienced when informally talking about researching gossip with academic colleagues. While there was no overt reference to malpractice or deception, there was an undercurrent of disquiet regarding publications and promotions, based on 'who you know', rather than the quality of your research and scholarship. It also illustrates ways in which the confidentiality of 'gossip as data' was maintained by using pseudonyms and a composite description. Addressing the ethical principle of confidentiality is a particular challenge for real-world research into gossip, and is considered next.

Protecting confidentiality

When authors describe their research, they are prohibited from disclosing confidential, personally identifiable information about research participants/organizations unless the person/organization has consented in writing, or there is legal authorization for doing so (APA Ethics Code Standard 4.07, n.d.). Researchers can protect confidentiality and ensure anonymity by using strategies to disguise some aspects of the data, so that neither participants nor third parties (e.g., employers, individuals/organizations being gossiped about) can be identified. The *APA Publication Manual* 7th ed. (2020) identifies four main strategies: (i) altering specific characteristics; (ii) limiting description of specific characteristics; (iii) disguising details by adding unrelated detail; and (iv) using composite descriptions. When using quotations taken from interview transcripts in qualitative studies, pseudonyms should also be used. Disguising identifying information, however, must be done carefully, as it is essential not to change content, or contextual information, that would lead readers to draw false conclusion (Sweeney et al., 2015). It is also important to note that the ethical requirement to protect confidentiality is entirely different to – and should not be confused with – dishonest and deceptive 'falsification' of research data that leads to retraction of articles. However, while guidance such as that provided by the APA is helpful, it does not necessarily provide a 'neat and tidy' solution to the ethical challenges of researching organizational gossip 'in situ', such as field studies, case studies, and auto/ethnography.

Ethical challenges

The ethical challenges of maintaining confidentiality in real-world research into gossip led Noon (2001) to suggest it may be an unresearchable topic. The challenges relate to covert 'eavesdropping' of conversations in public places and spaces, difficulties in obtaining informed consent, and the right to withdraw, particularly for absent third parties who may be unaware that they are the subject of gossip. These are also challenges ethnographers and autoethnographers face more generally when researching other topics, and which can cause research proposals to fall at the first hurdle of institutional review and research ethics committee approval – aptly described by Townsend et al. (2020, p. 366) as 'the IRB's stone wall'. However, Marzano (2018) argues that covert ethnographic research can be justified if a strictly deontological perspective is rejected in favour of one that centres on *social critique*.

Marzano's argument chimes both with that of Hasnas (2013, p. 280) 'not to privilege a deontological approach to ethics', and a critical management studies approach to critical theory and knowledge creation (Klikauer, 2015; Prasad et al., 2016).

Ethical challenges in practice

By way of an example, Box 4.2 illustrates the 'ethical can of worms' facing researchers seeking to better understand the everyday phenomenon of gossip in the workplace/organizations – however constituted. It is an extract of 'real-world' reviewer feedback (reproduced with permission) on a postdoctoral grant proposal I submitted for funding of further research into gossip and healthcare organizations.

BOX 4.2 AN ETHICAL CAN OF WORMS

This is an important and under-researched area. I do however have some reservations about the ethical aspects of the work. The study of gossip in organizations is surely an *ethical can of worms*, which cannot be wrapped up in two short paragraphs *that mainly focus on the research governance procedures of the applicant's institution*. I'd like to see at least two pages of A4 that *talk about ethics from the perspective of a reflexive researcher*, with examples of the sorts of problems that have come up in previous work on public sector gossip, and how the team has gone about addressing these.

Source: Extract from (anonymized) reviewer comments on a postdoctoral grant proposal, emphasis added.

Box 4.2 reflects my thinking and understanding of research ethics and researcher reflexivity 15 years ago; it is also an example of very helpful and constructive reviewer feedback. It is included here for the benefit of 'novice' researchers – who may be experienced researchers but 'new' to the field of organizational gossip, as well as early career researchers. The idiom 'to open a can of worms' means a complex, troublesome situation that arises when a decision or action produces considerable subsequent problems. The reviewer's 'can of worms' comment in Box 4.2 illustrates the complex relationship between procedural ethics of institutional and professional research codes and guidelines, and the need for reflexive research. The grant proposal was unsuccessful, which is not unusual; failed funding applications are an inevitable aspect of academic life. The important point for me was not to take the feedback personally, but to critically reflect on the grant proposal and reviewer feedback in reflexive conversations with colleagues, based on reflexive principles of:

- Acknowledging the constitutive nature of our research conversations.
- Adopting multi-perspective practices.
- Questioning and challenging our own intellectual assumptions.
- Making sense of actions in practical and responsive ways (Waddington, 2010, p. 312).

These conversations shaped – and indeed continue to do so – my reflexive research practice, thinking, and scholarship. Cunliffe (2016, p. 741), reflecting on the relationship between reflexivity and ethics, comments:

> I am now even more convinced that reflexivity offers a way of foregrounding our moral and ethical responsibility for people and for the world around us, and that an important question for students, educators, managers, and leaders to discuss is: What does it mean to BE [sic] reflexive?

By way of an example of what *being reflexive* means for me, in the course of writing the book during the pandemic I have engaged in reflexive conversations with colleagues who have commented on draft chapters and questions. These have mainly taken place online via email, and below is some feedback on a draft of Chapter 5 regarding the reflexive principle of adopting *multi-perspective practices*; but also included here as a 'taster' of what follows in the final chapter:

> Lots of exciting stuff in there! Such as this sentence: 'Gossip often occurs around a symbolic space where people lean in.' Gossip and space – very interesting indeed! In which corners does the voice take on a different tone and volume …? In short, a closing chapter in which you open up an abundance of future research avenues! Some readers will perhaps be overwhelmed (and I also experienced that feeling at some points …). 'But hey! That's Kathryn Waddington! Take it or leave it. She has more to offer than you can digest – therefore you should reread her.' (Ad van Iterson, personal communication, 27 May 2021; reproduced with permission)

Being reflexive has led me to further thinking about creative solutions to the ethical challenges of researching organizational gossip.

Creative solutions

Hurdley (2010a, 2010b) conducted workplace ethnography of the corridors of a university building, using a variety of methods including interviews, field notes, audio recording and photographs. Her focus of attention was the 'material, spatialised, contingent practices that slide away unseen and unheard beneath the buzzing repetition of metaphor, icon and cliché' (Hurdley, 2010a, p. 46). This study is used as an exemplar here, because the ethical issues encountered in researching corridor encounters and interactions are similar to those facing researchers of gossip. Namely, the difficulties involved in transgressing public/private boundaries and entering dangerous territory as a researcher. As Hurdley (2010b, p. 518) comments:

> The very character of corridor interactions made the corridors themselves ethically problematic as a research topic, in terms of both observation and publication. They are both more private than the meeting room and more public. While walking the corridors as a member of the public or of the institution, I might repeat all I saw and heard; yet my sight and hearing became dangerous senses once I assumed the role of researcher.

With regard to the latter point, procedural ethical constraints resulted in gossip, rumour, backbiting, intimacy, and scheming being *removed* from the subsequent writing up of the ethnography. The creative solution for Hurdley was the evolved notion of 'unpeopled ethnography' (2010b, p. 517), which can be extended to the study of visual and material manifestations of gossip. Other researchers have addressed the challenges and ethical dilemmas regarding related parties who feature in autoethnographic research through use of vignettes, dramatic episodes, and poetry. These can provide 'representations of experience without directly naming or fully describing them' (Haynes, 2018, p. 27). Lahman et al. (2019) used poetry to reflexively explore their experiences with an institutional review board, and perspectives of being evaluated by reviewers and chairs of IRB in their research with vulnerable groups such as lesbian, gay, bisexual, transgender, queer, questioning, and ally (LGBTQQA+) participants. While not directly related to the ethics of researching gossip, the following short poem illustrates the challenges facing researchers choosing 'unconventional' or 'challenging' research topics and methods.

What I do is research too
Interviewing queer youth
about their coming out experiences.

That's not research, says the dean.
You're going to have to do …
A survey, I ask?
Sure, that works.

(Poem by Eric Teman, in Lahman et al., 2019, p. 206;
reproduced with permission)

Engagement with different poetic structures and ways of conveying text
and voice is just one example of *how* researchers can actively, and critically, reflect upon the confines of bureaucratic, procedural ethics, in order
to develop depth and richness of insight. The complex relationship between
procedural ethics of disciplinary, institutional, and professional research
codes and guidelines *and* real-world research practice highlights the need
for reflexive ethics which is considered next.

Ethics and reflexivity

Reflexivity has traditionally fallen within the realm of qualitative research
and is sometimes dismissed (mainly by researchers/scholars steeped in a
quantitative, positivist paradigm) as 'navel-gazing' (Waddington, 2010).
But as Lumsden (2019) argues, reflexivity is *not* about 'navel-gazing' and
reflecting on the story and experiences of the researcher; rather, it is more
about the way in which knowledge is co-constructed with research participants. Reflexivity permeates every aspect of the research process, challenging us to be more fully conscious of the ideology, culture, and politics of
those we study and those we select as our audience(s).

The ethical requirement for high-quality research practice extends to all
research paradigms and methods. Reflexivity extends beyond minimalist
procedural ethics, to which all researchers are bound, to embrace and include
an *aspirational* ethical stance (Lahman et al., 2011). Examples of aspirational ethics include *relational ethics* (Hopner & Liu, 2020); *feminist ethics*
(Lindemann, 2019); *an ethics of care* (Gilligan, 1982/2009); and *ethics in
practice* (Clegg & van Iterson, 2009; Guillemin & Gilliam, 2004). These
aspirational ethical positions can be brought together under the umbrella
term of culturally responsive research. Culturally responsive researchers
are mindful that participants may have different, multiple, and conflicting
perspectives about reality, language, society, power, and knowledge.

Culturally responsive research

The chapter began with the argument that gossip can be positioned in the
field of applied social epistemology, which is characterized by a concern

for the relevance of ordinary events of everyday life. This is in contrast to my 'home' discipline of psychology, where a natural science epistemology still dominates, and relationships between the researcher and the researched are usually hierarchical and transactional and bound in procedural and legal ethics. This narrow view of ethics 'fails to account for issues of power and privilege, as well as inequalities in economic and sociocultural structures' (Hopner & Liu, 2020, p. 1). Stahl et al. (2019), writing from a psychological standpoint of neuroscience and information and communication technologies (ICTs), which are used for the collection and analysis of large neuroscientific data sets, also argue that the main problem with current approaches to research ethics is that:

> To some degree it achieves the opposite of what ethics should do. Instead of opening up, questioning and debating ethical questions, it closes them down and removes them from critical scrutiny. Furthermore, it *removes reflection upon ethical issues* from the research process and *makes shared forms of responsibility impossible.* (p. 9, emphasis added)

This critique from a psychological standpoint has wider relevance to business and management research, which has also been dominated by positivism and procedural ethics. As Jeanes (2017, p. 176) comments in regard to management and organization research, 'ethical committees are potentially irrelevant and/or dangerous to researchers and research quality'. Cunliffe and Ivaldi (2020, p. 294) address these critiques with a call to locate organizational codes of ethics *in practice*, and in local values, developing the idea of 'embedded ethics'. This is a form of 'lived ethics' in which researchers come to understand a sense, or feeling, for issues in their reflexive dialogue around narratives that reveal and explore ethical tensions. While Stahl et al. (2019, p. 5) suggest that Habermas's (1996) *discourse ethics* 'constitutes an ethical theory that is conducive to our interest in overcoming the perceived limitations of the IRB tradition'. It is clearly beyond the scope of this chapter – as it comes to an end – to discuss embedded ethics and discourse ethics in the depth they deserve. However, I suggest that as process-oriented approaches that focus on *reflexive dialogue*, they have potential as an additional aspirational ethical stance for future interdisciplinary gossip-related research. This represents a starting point from which to move beyond traditional and individual-centred views of ethics, to ones where agency and responsibility are distributed across various stakeholders. A reflexive dialogical approach to ethics offers another way to move beyond oppressive box-ticking of procedural ethics and is conducive with the scholarship of gossip as discourse, critical management studies, and culturally responsive research methodologies that:

> Challenge all forms of traditional paradigms [and] encourage instead a research stance where establishing respectful relationships with participants is central to both human dignity and the research. (Berryman et al., 2013, p.1)

Practice Point 4.1 summarizes what doing culturally responsive research entails.

Practice Point 4.1

Culturally responsive research

- Embeds relational ethics that consider care and compassion in research relationships.
- Adopts ethical reflexivity and an awareness of the impact of epistemology, language, culture, and power in the research process.
- Questions findings derived solely from societies that are white, educated, industrialized, rich, democratic (WEIRD).

The critique of findings derived from 'WEIRD' societies and populations has its roots in psychological research (Henrich, 2020). The suggestion is that such populations are individualistic, professionalized, and achievement oriented – characteristics that take preference over the importance of relationships, social roles, and responsibilities. Criticism is targeted particularly towards studies that rely upon US undergraduate students for their participant database (Masuda et al., 2020). This critique can be extended to laboratory-based studies of gossip with student populations (e.g., Feinberg et al., 2012; Sommerfeld et al., 2007). From an ethical standpoint of *beneficence* (doing good), research should only be carried out if some sort of benefit or good can be derived from it, for example, in terms of contribution to knowledge and wider organizational/social impact. Therefore, the question of whether or not a research study is worth undertaking should always be uppermost in researchers' minds. Furthermore, some journals – for example, the *Journal of Occupational and Organizational Psychology* – decline to publish papers based entirely on non-working populations, in other words, students. There is obviously editorial discretion to publish this type of paper if relevance and generalizability to working populations can be demonstrated. Future research will need to be ethically sound and, I suggest, should:

- Challenge reductionist methods and methodology.
- Discard the dismantling of gossip into narrow definitions and variables.
- Strive towards imaginative and innovative methodologies and methods.

Conclusion: some pointers for future research

This chapter has set out broad ethical principles for researching organizational gossip, with an emphasis on reflexive, relational ethics, and culturally responsive research practice. These are particularly relevant for future research focusing on gossip as a process of organizational communication and knowledge, rather than as an interpersonal/group process that focuses solely on the gossip triad. As an evolving area of research, the field of organizational gossip is arguably well placed to meet the European Research Council's (ERC) *Horizon 2020* research and innovation initiative. The ERC (n.d.):

> Supports frontier research, cross disciplinary proposals and pioneering ideas in new and emerging fields which introduce unconventional and innovative approaches. The ERC's mission is to encourage the highest quality research in Europe through competitive funding and to support investigator-driven frontier research across all fields of research, on the basis of scientific excellence. (p. 2)

Chapter 3 argued that critical participatory action research (Kemmis et al., 2014) was a suitable approach for future research, and importantly, Lindhult (2019, p. 6) argues:

> A core impetus of participatory and action research is making science relevant and useful for solving pressing problems and improving social conditions, and enabling stakeholders to participate in research and development processes.

Lindhult's argument complements the discourse ethics and dialogical approaches outlined above. He also argues that the criteria for judging 'scientific excellence' need to be reconstructed, based on a praxis-oriented epistemology inspired by pragmatism. This is a promising direction for future research, especially mixed methods research, which draws upon a pragmatic paradigm (Tashakkori et al., 2021). As discussed in Chapter 1, the coronavirus pandemic, lockdowns, and working from home have unexpectedly revealed gaps in organizational spaces and places that were previously filled by gossip. Furthermore, the rise in 'pandemic poetry' has highlighted the innovative role of arts-based research in the creation of socially useful knowledge and public scholarship. These are also important directions for future research. But new research pathways don't just form by themselves – 'we have to blaze the trails we want to pursue and that will be traveled [sic] by others' (Leavy, 2020, p. 320) – which is the focus of the following and final chapter.

References

Academy of Management (AOM) (n.d.). *AOM code of ethics* [online]. Available at: https://aom.org/about-aom/governance/ethics/code-of-ethics [Accessed 15th July 2021].

Adkins, K. (2017). *Gossip, epistemology, and power: Knowledge underground.* Cham: Palgrave Macmillan/Springer.

American Psychological Association (APA) (2020). *Publication manual* (7th ed.) Washington, DC: APA.

American Psychological Association (APA) (n.d.). *Ethical principles of psychologists and code of conduct* [online]. Available at: https://www.apa.org/ethics/code [Accessed 15th July 2021].

American Psychological Association (APA) (n.d.). *Ethics code 4.07: Use of confidential information for didactic and other purposes* [online]. Available at: https://www.apa.org/monitor/apr05/ethics [Accessed 15th July 2021].

Ayim, M. (1994). Knowledge through the grapevine: Gossip as inquiry. In R. F. Goodman & A. Ben-Ze'ev (Eds.), *Good gossip* (pp. 85–99). Kansas, KS: University Press of Kansas.

Bartolutti, T., & Magnani, L. (2019). Gossip. In D. Coady, & J. Chase (Eds.), *The Routledge handbook of applied epistemology* (pp. 272–283). Abingdon: Routledge.

Bell, E., Meriläinen, S., Taylor, S., & Tiernari, J. (2016). An ethic of care within critical management studies? In A., Prasad, P. Prasad, A.J. Mills, & J. Helms Mills (Eds.), *The Routledge companion to critical management studies* (pp. 56–68). Abingdon: Routledge.

Ben-Ze'ev, A. (1994). The vindication of gossip. In R. F. Goodman & A. Ben-Ze'ev (Eds.), *Good gossip* (pp. 11–24). Kansas, KS: University Press of Kansas.

Berryman, M., SooHoo, S., & Nevin, A. (2013). Culturally responsive methodologies from the margins. In M. Berryman, S. SooHoo, & A. Nevin (Eds.), *Culturally responsive methodologies* (pp. 1–33). Bingley: Emerald.

Boehm, C. (2019). Gossip and reputation in small-scale societies: A view from evolutionary anthropology. In F. Giardini, & R. Wittek (Eds.), *The Oxford handbook of gossip and reputation* (pp. 253–274). New York: Oxford University Press.

Clegg, S. R., & van Iterson, A. (2009). Dishing the dirt: Gossiping in organizations. *Culture and Organization, 15*(3–4), 275–289. doi: 10.1080/14759550903119293

Coady, J., & Chase, D. (2019). The return of applied epistemology. In D. Coady, & J. Chase (Eds.), *The Routledge handbook of applied epistemology* (pp. 3–12). Abingdon: Routledge.

Cunliffe, A. L. (2016). "On becoming a critically reflective practitioner" redux: What does it mean to *be* reflexive? *Journal of Management Education, 490*(6), 740–746. doi: 10.1177/1052562916668919

Cunliffe, A. L., & Ivaldi, S. (2020). Embedded ethics and reflexivity: Narrating a charter of ethical experience. *Management Learning, 52*(3), 294–310. doi: 10.1177/1350507620960014

De Backer, C. J. S., Van den Bulck, H., Fisher, M. L., & Ouvrein, G. (2019). Gossip and reputation in the media. In F. Giardini, & R. Wittek (Eds.), *The Oxford handbook of gossip and reputation* (pp. 325–342). New York: Oxford University Press.

de Sousa, R. (1994). In praise of gossip: Indiscretion as a saintly virtue. In R. F. Goodman & A. Ben-Ze'ev (Eds.), *Good gossip* (pp. 25–33). Kansas, KS: University Press of Kansas.

Duignan, B. (n.d.). *Utilitarianism* [online]. Available at: https://www.britannica.com/topic/utilitarianism-philosophy [Accessed 15th July 2021].

European Research Council (n.d.). *Horizon 2020* [online]. Available at: https://ec.europa.eu/programmes/horizon2020/en/h2020-section/european-research-council [Accessed 15th July 2021].

Feinberg, M., Willer, R., Stellar, J., & Keltner, D. (2012). The virtues of gossip: Reputational information sharing as prosocial behavior. *Journal of Personality and Social Psychology, 102*(5), 1015–1030. doi: 10.1037/a0026650

Gabriel, Y. (2018). Stories and narratives. In C. Cassell, A. L. Cunliffe, & G. Grandy (Eds.), *The SAGE handbook of qualitative business and management research methods* (pp. 63–81). London: SAGE Publications.

Gilligan, C. (1982/2009). *In a different voice*. Cambridge, MA: Harvard University Press.

Goodman, R. F., & Ben-Ze'ev, A. (Eds.) (1994). *Good gossip*. Kansas, KS: University Press of Kansas.

Guillemin, M., & Gillam, L. (2004). Ethics, reflexivity, and "ethically important moments" in research. *Qualitative Inquiry, 10*(2), 261–280. doi: 10.1177/1077800403262360

Habermas, J. (1996). *Between facts and norms: Contributions to a discourse theory of law and democracy* (translated by W. Rehg). Cambridge, MA: MIT Press.

Hasnas, J. (2013). Teaching business ethics: The principles approach, *Journal of Business Ethics Education, 10*, 275–304. doi: 10.5840/bee20131014

Haynes, K. (2018). Autoethnography. In C. Cassell, A. L. Cunliffe, & G. Grandy (Eds.), *The SAGE handbook of qualitative business and management research methods* (pp. 17–31). London: SAGE Publications.

Heidegger, M. (1962). *Being and time*. New York: Harper & Row.

Henrich, J. (2020). *The weirdest people in the world*. London: Allen Lane.

Hopner, V., & Liu, J. H. (2020). Relational ethics and epistemology: The case for complementary first principles in psychology. *Theory and Psychology, 31*(2), 179–198. doi: 10.1177/0959354320974103

Hurdley, R. (2010a). The power of corridors: Connecting doors, mobilising materials, plotting openness. *The Sociological Review, 58*(1), 45–64. doi: 10.1111/j.1467-954X.2009.01876.x

Hurdley, R. (2010b). In the picture or off the wall? Ethical regulation, research habitus, and unpeopled ethnography. *Qualitative Inquiry, 16*(6), 417–528. doi: 10.1177/1077800410370676

Issa, T., & Pick, D. (2010). Ethical mindsets: An Australian study. *Journal of Business Ethics, 96*, 613–629. doi:10.1007/s10551-010-0487-0

Jeanes, E. (2017). Are we ethical? Approaches to ethics in business and management research. *Organization, 24*(2), 1754–197. doi: 10.1177/1350508416656930

Kemmis, S., McTaggart, R., & Nixon, R. (Eds.), (2014). *The action research planner: Doing critical participatory action research.* Cham: Springer.

Klikauer, T. (2015). Critical management studies and critical theory: A review. *Capital & Class, 39*(2), 197–220. doi: 10.1177/0309816815581773

Kniffin, K.M., & Wilson, D.S. (2005). Utilities of gossip across organizational levels: Multilevel selection, free-riders, and teams. *Human Nature, 16*(3), 278–292. doi: 10.1007/s12110-005-1011-6.pdf

Kniffin, K.M., & Wilson, D.S. (2010). Evolutionary perspectives on workplace gossip: Why and how gossip can serve groups. *Group & Organization Management, 35*(2), 150–176. doi: 10.1177/1059601109360390

Lahman, M. K. E., Geist, M. R., Rodriguez, K. L., Graglia, P., & DeRoche, K. K. (2011). Culturally responsive relational reflexive ethics in research: The three rs. *Qual Quant, 45*, 1397–1414. doi: 10.1007/s11135-010-9347-3

Lahman, M. K. E, Teman, E., & Richard, V. M. (2019). IRB as poetry, *Qualitative Inquiry, 25*(2), 200–214. doi: 10.1177/1077800417744580

Lawrence, T. B., & Maitlis, S. (2012). Care and possibility: Enacting and ethic of care through narrative practice. *Academy of Management Review, 37*(4), 641–663. doi: 10.5465/amr20100466

Leavy, P. (2020). *Method meets art: Arts-based research practice.* New York: The Guildford Press.

Lindemann, H. (2019). *An invitation to feminist ethics* (2nd ed.) New York: Oxford University Press.

Lindhult, E. (2019). Scientific excellence in participatory and action research: Part I rethinking research quality. *Technology Innovation Management Review, 9*(5), 6–21. doi: 10.22215/timreview/1237

Lumsden, K. (2019). *Reflexivity: Theory, method, and practice.* Abingdon: Routledge.

Marzano, M. (2018). The ethics of covert ethnographic research. In C. I. Macleod, J. Marx, P. Mnyaka, & Treharne, G. J. (Eds.), *The Palgrave handbook of ethics in critical research* (pp. 399–414). Cham: Palgrave Macmillan.

Masuda, T., Batdor, B., & Senzaki, S. (2020). Culture and attention: Future directions to expand research beyond the geographical regions of WEIRD cultures. *Frontiers in Psychology* [online]. Available at: 10.3389/fpsyg.2020.01394 [Accessed 15th July, 2021].

Mills, C. (2010). Experiencing gossip: The foundations for a theory of embedded organizational gossip. *Group & Organization Management, 35*(2), 213–240. doi: 10.1177/1059601109360392

National Health and Medical Research Council (2018). *Australian Code for Responsible Conduct of Research* [online]. Available at: www.nhmrc.gov.au/guidelines/publications/r41 [Accessed 15th July 2021].

Noon, M. (2001). Suggested revisions to Kurland and Pelled's model of gossip and power. *Academy of Management Review*, *26*(2), 173–174.

Prasad, A., Prasad, P., Mills, A. J., & Helms Mills, J. (2016). Debating knowledge: Rethinking critical management studies in a changing world. In A., Prasad, P. Prasad, A.J. Mills, & J. Helms Mills (Eds.), *The Routledge companion to critical management studies* (pp. 3–41). Abingdon: Routledge.

Sinner, A., Hasebe-Ludt, E., & Leggo, C. (2018). Long story short: Encounters with creative nonfiction as methodological provocation. In P. Leavy (Ed.), *Handbook of arts-based research* (pp. 165–189). New York: The Guildford Press.

Sommerfeld, R. D., Krambeck, H-J., Semmann, D., & Milinski, M. (2007). Gossip as an alternative for direct observation in games of indirect reciprocity. *Proceedings of the National Academy of Sciences*, *104*(44), 17435–17440. doi: 10.1073/pnas.0704598104

Stahl, B. B., Akintoye, S., Fothergill, B. T., Guerrero, M., Knight, W., & Ulnicane, I. (2019). Beyond research ethics: Dialogues in neuro-ICT research, 1–9. *Frontiers in Human Neuroscience* [online]. Available at: 10.3389/fnhum.2019.00105/full [Accessed 15th July 2021].

Sweeney, L., Crosas, M., & Bar-Sinai, M. (2015). Sharing sensitive data with confidence: The datatags system. *Technology Science* [online]. Available at: techscience.org/a/2015101601/ [Accessed 15th July 2021].

Tashakkori, A. M., Johnson, R. B., & Teddlie, C. (2021). *Foundations of mixed methods research: Integrating quantitative and qualitative approaches in the social and behavioural sciences* (2nd ed.) Thousand Oaks, CA: SAGE Publications.

Tassiello, V., Lombardi, S., & Costabile, M. (2018). Are we truly wicked when gossiping at work? The role of valence, interpersonal closeness and social awareness. *Journal of Business Research*, *84*, 141–149. doi: 10.1016/j.busres.2017.11.013

Tooman, T., Akinci, C., & Davies, H. (2016). Understanding knowledge and knowing. In K. Orr, S. Nutley, S. Russell, R. Bain, B. Hacking, & C. Moran (Eds.), *Knowledge and practice in business and organisations* (pp. 17–29). New York: Routledge.

Tourish, D. & Craig, R. (2020). Research misconduct in business and management studies: Causes, consequences and possible remedies. *Journal of Management Inquiry*, *29*(2), 174–187. doi: 10.1177/1056492618792621

Townsend, T. W, Duggins, A., Bragg, B., McCoy, T., Guerrault, J., Newell, J., & Tiberi, H. (2020). The IRB's stone wall: Rollercoaster of doom. In A. F. Hermann (Ed.). *The Routledge international handbook of organizational ethnography* (pp. 366–382). Abingdon: Routledge.

Vaidyanathan, B., Khalsa, S., & Ecklund, E. H. (2016). Gossip as social control: Informal sanctions on ethical violations in scientific workplaces. *Social Problems*, *63*(4), 554–572. doi: 10.1093/socpro/spw022

Waddington, K. (2010). Organisational gossip, sense-making and the spookfish: A reflexive account. *International Journal of Management Concepts and Philosophy*, *4*(2), 311–325. doi: 10.1501/IJMCP.2010.037815

Westacott, E. (2012). *The virtues of our vices: A modest defence of gossip, rudeness. And other bad habits.* Princeton, NJ: Princeton University Press.

5 Future directions and pathways to practice-based knowledge

Introduction: putting practice on the map

This chapter brings together and integrates themes and threads from previous chapters, setting out future directions and pathways for new approaches to practice-based knowledge and theory building. Overall, the aim is to put practice firmly on the map, focusing on the role of academic-practitioner relationships in the co-production of knowledge and practice-based research evidence (Bartunek & McKenzie, 2018; Fox, 2011). Chapter 1 highlighted the 'sentinel function' of gossip as an early warning indicator of future failure, which requires the creation of 'speak up cultures' (Reitz & Higgins, 2019):

> Speaking up and listening up matters in our organizations. Without it, you might only hear about misconduct and wrongdoing when it appears on the front page of the newspaper. It is vital for innovation and adapting to this latest age of upheaval. It is essential to motivation and engagement. (pp. i–xxxi)

This is an important direction for future research, for example, leading to new impacts for practice in studies of professional misconduct and counterproductive work behaviours (Marcus et al., 2016; Searle & Rice, 2020). This concluding chapter therefore speaks to a wide audience of readers including researchers, practitioners, managers, C-suite executives, senior independent directors, and business leaders. Academics and practitioners will need to 'travel light' in this evolving area of research. Things that need to be left behind include 'rigid baggage and frameworks from the past … and expectations of quick journeys with clear and tangible outcomes' (Nutley et al., 2016, p. 244). Things to be included are a focus on relationships,

DOI: 10.4324/9780367652982-5

use of abstract concepts, metaphors, and articulation of values that matter. Reflexivity and a practice lens are also essential items to pack.

Reflexivity

This was introduced in Chapter 1 and has been an integrative thread throughout the book. My reflexive position as an academic *and* a practitioner is one where I do not pretend to be value-neutral (Gabriel, 2015). Values of honesty, speaking up, compassion, and having the courage to 'swim against the tide' – meaning to not follow what everyone else is doing – have informed my research and writing decisions. My map has its foundations in research into the role of gossip in nursing and healthcare organizations and is shaped (but not led) by my 'home' discipline of work psychology, and identity as a 'practice-based academic'. I owe a debt of gratitude to my colleague and friend Philippa Sully, who introduced me to this term when I was struggling with my early academic identity and position in psychology, having arrived there from a practice-based pathway in healthcare. Kvernbekk and Jarning (2019) hypothesize that maps of scientific disciplines and fields of study serve two fundamental purposes. The first is to show the constitutive components in the discipline/field; the second is to indicate how these are connected, and to separate the mapped field from the 'lands beyond' (p. 560). In the future, the field of organizational gossip should extend to lands beyond the social sciences, organization, and communication studies, to include the role and contribution of arts-based research. From a reflexive practice perspective, arts-based research pays particular attention to issues of voice – 'we do not speak for others, nor do we give voice to others, as they already have their own voices, but we can use our platform as researchers to *amplify the voices* of others' (Leavy, 2020, p. 280, emphasis added).

Attention to voice is significant for research into gossip that includes practitioner, and other stakeholder perspectives, such as clients and service users. Research has focused on voice as a means of detecting errors, identifying safety issues, and exposing unethical behaviour such as harassment and bullying (e.g., Harlos & Knoll, 2021; Morrison, 2014). Future research in these areas will need to *adopt a practice lens* to produce useful knowledge.

Adopting a practice lens

Practice Point 5.1 outlines key features of a practice lens (Bain & Mueller, 2016), which is an essential orienting feature for future directions on the map of gossip, organization, and work.

Practice Point 5.1

Key features of a practice lens

- The social world is understood to consist of practices, activities, and performances.
- Practices involve bodily action, mental activity, and material things.
- Knowledge is understood differently, and knowing is a social phenomenon shared with others.

A practice lens can offer alternative insights into the *processual constitution* of organizations, which is a core theme in this book. Latham (2019), writing 'in praise of practice', comments on the supremacy of deductively derived theory, and research that is not actionable. He argues that existing theory should not dictate empirical questions and research methods; instead, 'real world questions should come first and theory and methods should follow' (p. 13). Business, organizational, and management research are most useful/valuable to society when the 'reality of practice truly informs theorizing' (Bartunek & McKenzie, 2018, p. 1). This is at the core of academic-practitioner relationships, co-production of knowledge, and creation of practice-based research evidence, which are considered next.

Academic-practitioner research into gossip: narratives about practice

One way of thinking about academic-practitioner research and relationships is to think in terms of creating narratives – or stories – about practice (Waddington et al., in press). Terminology used to reflect the work of academics and practitioners involved in this type of research is varied, including: 'practitioner-scientist' (Latham, 2019); 'scientist-practitioner' (Jex & Britt, 2014); 'scholar-practitioner' (Simón & Ferreiro, 2017); 'practitioner-scholar' (Buick et al., 2016). This can be confusing, reflecting conflicts and tensions between different disciplines, fields of research, and differences between academic-practitioner values, perspectives, and priorities. Bartunek and Rynes (2018, p. 81) observe that there is 'a considerable literature on the "academic-practitioner gap" in multiple social science disciplines'. The gap has its roots in conflicts and tensions between scholars and practitioners, with both parties shouldering part of the blame (Buick et al., 2016). Bartunek and Rynes's (2018, p. 85) analysis of empirical papers about academic-practitioner relationships revealed five distinct storylines, as outlined below.

1. *Contact stories*: academic-practitioner contact enhances both practitioner implementation of academic findings and citations of academic articles.
2. *Discrepancy stories*: differences in interests and values placed on research lead to discrepancies between academics and practitioners. This has often been found in HR.
3. *Culture stories*: fundamental differences in the underlying cultures of academics and practitioners foster tensions.
4. *Impact stories*: practitioner journals have more impact on academia than academic journals have on practice.
5. *Similarities stories*: exploration of interests and concerns shows that academic and practitioners are often similar to each other.

According to Bartunek and Rynes, the above storylines 'tell straightforward tales of similarities *or* differences' (p. 87). But it may not be quite so straightforward for academic-practitioner research into gossip, which I contend can be understood as weaving narratives about practice. This resonates with both: (a) the arts-based approach to future research advocated in the book; and (b) the strands of critical management studies on discourse and narrative addressed in Chapter 2.

Closing the academic-practitioner gap: weaving a narrative?

Bartunek and McKenzie (2018) argue that the often-used metaphor of an academic-practitioner 'gap' despite its ubiquity is outmoded, suggesting the term *interface* is a more appropriate metaphor. That is, a means or place of interaction between two systems, organizations, or groups: 'a meeting-point or common ground between two parties, or disciplines; also, interaction, liaison, dialogue' (p. 2).

Waddington and Kaplan (2021) created a shared narrative of reflexive co-facilitation of an action learning case study of organizational compassion in a UK university. In the case study, the metaphor of *interface* was extended to *intersection*, and academic-practitioner collaboration was described in terms of 'weaving a narrative' (p. 67). Burgelman et al. (2018), writing from a position of strategy process and practice research, identify three ways to see relationships and intersections between two perspectives/positions in academic-practitioner research: (i) *complimentary*, which acknowledges that each is examining different but compatible phenomena (comparable to the 'similarities' storyline in Table 5.1); (ii) *critical*, which argues that strategy process scholarship is of limited use in practice

Table 5.1 A template for critical reflection and future research

Suggested Probes	Identifying

• What issues lie beneath the narrative/episode?
• What is already known about these issues?
• What are the underlying emotions?
• What are the risks of not attending to gossip?
	Underlying issues
	Clarifying, focusing,
	  and reviewing the
	  evolving issues

• What are the organizational triggers?
• How and where is power manifest?
• Where are the 'pockets' of gossip?
• Who are the key gatekeepers and stakeholders?
	Context
	Exploring, discovering,
	  and revealing the
	  context

• Is the gossip informative, toxic, or harmless?
• Does the gossip contain risks to the organization/staff/others?
• What can be discarded?
• How do we judge the credibility of the content/source?
• What needs further verification from other sources?
• What/Where are gaps between knowledge sources?
	Nature of knowledge
	Revealing, amplifying,
	  and clarifying
	  information that may
	  require *action*

• How practical is it to use this knowledge from gossip?
• What are the risks and benefits associated with its use?
• What are the ethical implications of acting/not acting?
• How can this knowledge be integrated with other sources?
	Actions
	Disseminating and
	  integrating with other
	  sources of knowledge

Source: Updated and amended from Waddington (2012, p. 156).

(comparable to the 'discrepancy storyline'); and (iii) *combinatory*, in which the two perspectives/positions:

> Can be synthesized into a single, coherent body of research ... enhanced by the recent development of a strong *process ontology* in which everything is seen as process, reflecting continuous activity. (Burgelman et al., 2018, p. 540, emphasis added)

A combinatory view brings a new *intertwined* storyline to academic-practitioner relationships, reflected in the metaphor of *weaving a narrative*. The art of weaving is the creation of fabric using intersecting threads and materials. This metaphor can be extended to include reflexive methodology in regard to weaving empirical materials in interdisciplinary and mixed methods research (Alvesson & Sköldberg, 2018; McChesney & Aldridge, 2019). This could of course be hindered, or indeed unravelled, by 'disciplinary imperialism' (Green & Andersen, 2019, p. 727) – where standards from one academic/practice discipline are uncritically applied to new fields without recognition of the potential for new insights and fresh thinking. However, I suggest an integrated metaphor of *intersections and weaving a narrative* can redirect research away from binary methods, and rigid paradigmatic associations and/or assumptions, towards an interdisciplinary research agenda.

The changing landscape of work: trends for future research

As discussed in Chapter 1, the changing landscape of work, and outcomes of the coronavirus pandemic, will inevitably impact questions relating to where, with whom, why, and how does gossip occur in contemporary work environments and organizations. Microsoft's (2021) *Work Trend Index* suggests that hybrid work environments – a blended model where some employees return to the workplace and others continue to work from home – will shape the future landscape of work. The report identifies seven 'urgent trends that every business leader *needs to know*' (Microsoft, 2021, p. 2, emphasis added):

1. Flexible work is here to stay.
2. Leaders are out of touch with employees and need a wake-up call.
3. High productivity is masking an exhausted workforce.
4. Generation Z is at risk and will need to be re-energized.
5. Shrinking networks are endangering innovation.
6. Authenticity will spur productivity and well-being.
7. Talent is everywhere in a hybrid work world.

A central argument in this book is that gossip as a communicative practice and process is a pathway to organizational knowledge. Paying attention to gossip from an academic-practitioner research perspective can provide a 'wake-up call' that leaders need to *hear*, and co-created knowledge will be needed to address the other urgent trends identified above. As van Iterson et al. (2011) argued a decade ago, the organizational 'underlife' enacted in and through gossip represents aspects of culture 'that members of an organization, *including its leaders, should pay attention to, and to ignore this can be fatal*' (p. 388, emphasis added). Looking ahead, the Microsoft (2021) report also recommends rebuilding social capital and culture as priority areas:

> *Rebuilding social capital is a business imperative*: Leaders should also encourage and reward managers to build social capital at work … *Cultivating a culture of kindness*, fun, and *cooperative collaboration* is

just as important to the bottom line ... being nice to each other, chatting with each other [are part of work]. They feed productivity and nurture the soil from which people will produce ideas. (p. 30, emphasis added)

There is a clear role for future research here because, firstly, social capital, which in essence is about benefits derived from social interactions (see Lin et al., 2017), is relevant in research that addresses gossip from relational and/or group perspectives (e.g., Ben-Hador, 2019; Ellwardt et al., 2012). Secondly, cultivating a culture of kindness is also relevant for future research into gossip from a moral and ethical standpoint. Kindness and compassion are two vital human values, and aside from other moral values are the 'foundation of *social and personal relationships*' (Shea & Lionis, 2017, p. 457, emphasis added).

Evidence is emerging that 'muted dialogue' and 'critical corridor talk' (Jameson, 2019, p. 280) – which are arguably gossip by another name – play an important role in informal leadership and kindness. The 'contours of kindness' (Haskins et al., 2018, p. 29) are to be found in trust, compassion, and teamwork. Arguably, contours of kindness are also found in teams that demonstrate high levels of 'psychological safety' (Edmondson, 1999), and more widely in psychologically safe work environments. Newman et al.'s (2017) systematic review found that these are environments where:

Employees feel safe to voice ideas, willingly seek feedback, provide honest feedback, collaborate, take risks and experiment ... psychological safety was identified as the number one characteristic of successful high-performing teams [and] psychological safety is especially important in work environments where employee and customer safety are paramount, such as the healthcare or aviation industries, as it has been shown to be critical in reducing employee errors and enhancing safety. (p. 521)

Thus, exploration of the links – and lines – between psychological safety, gossip, and compassion is a potentially significant area for future research and is considered next.

Gossip, compassion, and psychological safety

Compassion science (Seppälä et al., 2017) and the evidence-base for the benefits of organizational compassion (see Box 5.1) point to significant benefits for individuals, teams, businesses, and organizations.

BOX 5.1 THE EVIDENCE-BASE FOR ORGANIZATIONAL COMPASSION

- Those who experience compassionate leadership at work are more likely to report an emotional commitment to their organization and to talk about it in positive terms.
- Compassion breeds compassion – those who experience compassion are then more likely to demonstrate it towards others.
- Managers who perceive that their organization values their well-being are more likely to show supportive behaviour towards the people they manage.
- There are mutual benefits: (i) for people receiving compassion; (ii) the person demonstrating compassion; and (iii) also colleagues who witness compassionate acts.
- Experiencing compassion at work: (i) reduces employee turnover and increases organizational citizenship; and (ii) connects co-workers psychologically and results in a stronger bond between them.
- Relationships based upon compassion are stronger, more positive, and collaborative.
- People working in compassionate organizations are less likely to experience stress and burnout.
- Compassion can also help with growing trust between individuals and creates psychological safety.
- This can create a willingness to discuss and learn from errors and failures, talking about them more easily, and learning from those mistakes.
- Compassionate cultures can result in improved innovation and creativity.
- Compassionate cultures are better able to appreciate and value diversity, including cognitively diverse contributions.
    Source: Compiled from Poorkavoos (2016, 2017); Seppälä et al. (2017); West (2021); Worline and Dutton (2017).

The evidence-base for compassion in Box 5.1, coupled with the evaluative component of gossip as an expression of care and concern, and an ethic of care as discussed in Chapter 4, suggests that the relationship between gossip and compassion is worthy of further consideration.

Gossip and compassion

While the relationship between gossip and compassion might at first seem a little incongruous, they both share an evolutionary history. As outlined in Chapter 2, Dunbar (1996) has argued that *language evolved* to enable people to gossip and exchange socially useful information. To summarize, a key argument from evolutionary social science, which draws predominantly from psychology and anthropology, is that gossip is an indirect form of social control and regulation. For instance, to address the problem of free riders, who are individuals who take the benefits of group activities without reciprocating. Gossip is an *adapted emotional reaction* against social isolation and perceived unfairness/injustice (Beersma & Van Kleef, 2012; Boehm, 2019). Kniffin and Wilson (2010, p. 170) state simply that gossip is 'a central, evolved part of how people in organizations communicate with each other'. Similarly, compassion has been framed as a 'discrete and *evolved emotional experience* ... conceived as a state of concern for the suffering or unmet need of another, coupled with a desire to alleviate that suffering' (Goetz & Simon-Thomas, 2017, p. 3, emphasis added).

Gilbert (2021) argues that compassion can be understood from an analysis of evolved resource-regulation strategies – referred to as care and share versus control and hold – which occurred in small hunter-gatherer groups. In these groups, individualistic, self-promoting control and hold strategies, such as trying to secure and accumulate more than others, were shunned and shamed. Conversely, caring and sharing lifestyles created social contexts for the evolution of new forms of complex human competencies such as '*language*, reasoning, planning, empathy, and self-awareness' (Gilbert, 2021, p. 1, emphasis added). There are, I contend, opportunities and avenues for future research into gossip and compassion in the workplace. The evolved resource-regulation strategies of *care and share* versus *control and hold* may also prove to be useful metaphors with which to understand 21st-century business environments. Nevertheless, uncritical adoption of an 'evolutionary lens' is also problematic. Nicholson (2010) argues that evolutionary psychology is central to core processes of work – how we organize, coordinate, and direct human activity towards collective goals. Saad (2011, 2020) is also an advocate of an evolutionary lens in the business sciences but notes its 'image problem amongst marketing scholars' (2020, p. 485). Recurring criticisms that have tarnished the evolutionary lens fall into two distinct camps: (i) ideological, concerning the use of evolutionary thinking to support extreme right-wing political ideologies; and (ii) epistemological, concerning unfalsifiable hypotheses generated via principles of evolutionary psychology. While these may be due, in part, to conceptual misunderstandings, there are also serious and legitimate concerns, but which are beyond the remit of this chapter and book. The important point to note here is that an evolutionary lens is *not the only one* with which to explore the intertwined phenomena of gossip and compassion. I contend that the lens of psychological safety also offers some promising pathways for future research.

Psychological safety

Compassionate work cultures are more likely to have high levels of psychological safety, where staff are more likely to speak up if they have concerns, and compassionate leadership skills of attending, understanding, empathizing, and helping are vital (West, 2021). The role of gossip as a response to perceived unfairness/injustice is key; psychological safety is characterized by team climates of inclusivity, interpersonal trust, and mutual respect. The need for psychological safety is clearly paramount in healthcare, and high-reliability organizations such as aviation, chemical industries, and nuclear power operations (Serou et al., 2021). While for Google:

> Psychological safety is viewed as the most important aspect of a team's dynamics, and teams that demonstrate higher levels of psychological safety have been shown to achieve higher sales numbers. (Wisdom & Wei, 2017, cited in Swendiman et al., 2019, p. 234)

Arguably, attending to concerns expressed as gossip, and an open-minded approach might be a way of signalling the level of psychological safety there is in both the team and the wider organizational culture. There are three key academic-practitioner points to note here. Firstly, the role of gossip in groups and networks, as evidenced in academic research (e.g., Beersma et al., 2019; Ellwardt, 2019); secondly, the role of professional/practitioner networks in facilitating the exchange of knowledge 'through reciprocal, mutually supportive relationships, where aspects of trust, interdependence, and reputation are key' (Dixon-Wood, 2019, p. 54). Finally, the potential for shared academic-practitioner research narratives that could explore further the positive role of gossip as a means of developing and maintaining psychologically safe 'speak up' and 'listen up' team and organizational cultures (Hughes, 2019). There is also another angle that could be explored further. That is, speaking up – and being heard and supported from a position of psychological safety and compassion – about harmful aspects of gossip as bullying, microaggression, and abuse of power in organizations (e.g., Farley, 2019; Pheko, 2018).

Future directions for gossip and compassion

Jameson's (2019) mixed methods (but predominantly qualitative) research used the higher education lens of 'critical being' – which embodies thinking, self-reflection, and action – to theorize ways academics find relief from neoliberal, economically driven 'command and control' management. Kindness was found in the background, in the 'critical corridor talk' of informal leaders:

> This is a secret language of dialogic resistance, to be found under the radar, tucked away in the blindspots of formally recognized communication … such 'understage' dialogical spaces [are] like a soft, repetitive reminder of the need for human values. (Jameson, 2019, p. 279)

Jameson's research addressed the questions: 'How and why do academic staff talk to each other with kindness to support mutual survival from experiences in higher education? Is this just gossip?' (2019, p. 282).

Is this just gossip?

The question '*is this just gossip*' reflects the public face of gossip, and the widespread negative stereotypes, perceptions, and definitions that can be problematic for researchers (Waddington, 2012). It reveals the tensions, difficulties, and differences, when talking and writing about gossip as it is experienced in practice, and gossip as it is written about in academia. But it is also important to acknowledge the positive side of gossip:

> Yes, I think gossip can be positive in the compassionate sense you outline, and there is a debate to be had about whether it is helpful or not to call it 'gossip'. I suppose I wanted in those works to distinguish critical corridor talk from gossip within an academic environment in particular (given that part of our academic role is critical thinking, knowledge-generation and reflection), but you can equally make an argument the other way, so I think it's borderline. For me, specifying the critical corridor talk edge of that borderline was important, but it's always possible to define other edges and ways of looking at this. *Interesting debate*! (Jill Jameson, personal communication, 4 May 2021; reproduced with permission)

Jameson's (2019) research also reflects the paradox of gossip, which is that order to be useful, gossip *has to be* publicly condemned and occur 'below the radar' (Waddington, 2012, p. 23). Attempts to sanitize or legitimize gossip as sanctioned or 'professionalized' talk may simply eradicate its value and utility. What is important then is to find ways of uncovering and understanding the *processes and flows* of gossip as it circulates around and between organizations. A critical 'narrative lens' on compassion (Frost et al., 2006, p. 845), which highlights the way that lived experience is captured, curated, and communicated in storied ways, offers a way of uncovering and understanding gossip. However, the question '*is/was this just gossip*' – in other words, superfluous and trivial talk – remains a critical one.

Was this just gossip?

Haroun's (2021) account of a UK 'Doctors in the woods project' also points to the role that gossip plays in kindness and compassion. A group of junior doctors spent time on a short off-grid (no Wi-Fi, no emails, no mobile phone connection) nature and resilience retreat in Somerset. The intention was to support their well-being, resilience, and self-compassion, using nature as a facilitation space, and which involved carrying out a conservation task of pruning knotweed from Douglas fir trees, as described below:

> They worked in small groups quickly and swiftly … After some time, the work slowed to a steadier pace, and conversations began to emerge about the challenges of being a doctor … [Later] that evening under the forest canopy a fire was lit and the doctors sat in a circle around it as generations of human beings have done before in this ancient ritual … They shared personal experiences about the emotional strain of being a doctor; and as each one talked the others listened and witnessed all the time looking at the fire … The doctors spoke stories of shame into the glowing flame, a good place to send them. (Haroun, 2021, p. 111)

As editor of the book where the 'Doctors in the woods project' featured (Waddington, 2021), I was curious to know more about the 'campfire conversations', so I asked Justin Haroun: *Was this just gossip?*

> I am not sure, but something did strike me about the space where this fireside conversation was happening. Gossip often occurs around a symbolic space where people lean in. There was also a sense of sharing in an informal way to ease the pain of powerlessness. Gossip when practiced by those lower down the hierarchical structure seems

to me is often a way to help the powerless regain some agency. That was happening around the fire as nameless predators were discussed with full knowledge of who they were. The sharing seemed to give the group a sense of strength to carry on and bear the system. (Justin Haroun, personal communication, 8 January 2021; reproduced with permission)

Jameson's (2019) account of critical corridor talk, and the importance of creating spaces for kindness; and Haroun's (2021) account of junior doctors' compassionate conversations around the campfire are important for future research for at least three reasons. Firstly, they foreground practice over predetermined theory; or as Haroun asserts: 'Start by walking the terrain of compassion – practice – then move to studying the map – theory' (p. 113). Secondly, they illustrate the pragmatic challenges of working with gossip as a prototypical category lacking clear-cut boundaries; but this also makes gossip an interesting topic to research and develop practice-based theory. Reflecting on many academic conversations, emails (e.g., from Jill Jameson above), and interview data, the most frequent response I get when talking about – or inquiring into – gossip is: '*How interesting!*' For example, I asked participants what their first thoughts and impressions were when invited to take part in research interviews about their experiences of gossip in hospital settings. Below is a typical response – emphasis added:

Hmmm, I thought it was *really interesting* and it just *got me thinking* about the notion of gossip a little bit, *I hadn't really thought about it before*, it's a naturally occurring phenomenon, and there it is, it did actually *trigger* some thought. (Waddington, 2012, p. 139)

As Weick (1989, p. 525) observed, 'when one reacts with the feeling *that's interesting*, that reaction is a clue that … past understanding has been found inadequate'. A third reason to conduct further research into gossip and compassion is the potential to reveal and hear 'hidden narratives' from marginalized voices. According to Frost et al. (2006), when we look through the lens of compassion as narrative, the often hidden and 'dark side' of organization comes into focus. This is an important direction for future research, potentially leading to impacts for practice in areas relating to: (i) counterproductive work behaviours; (ii) professional misconduct; and (iii) creation of speak up and listen up cultures.

Implications and impact for practice: is this *just gossip*?

The human values of kindness and compassion are clearly related to gossip as evaluative talk when the talk expresses care and/or concern from a moral and ethical standpoint (see also Chapter 4). This can be constituted as *'just gossip'*; in other words, based on and acting according to what is morally right and fair. This should include talk that extends beyond that which is only about absent third parties (i.e. individuals and groups); gossip is not merely, nor simply, inter/personal in nature. Adkins (2017, p. 9), reflecting upon her research experience of collecting gossip narratives and episodes, comments:

> When we gossip, we aren't always just talking about people (let alone the behind their back part) ... people gossip at work a lot, and often what they're talking about (evaluatively, confidentially, sometimes angrily) are corporate or institutional events and [in]actions, which is not reducible to the personalities of the actors.

Critical reflection upon gossip about corporate/institutional events, and inactions – in other words, failure to attend to the early warning signals expressed in gossip – is, I suggest, important and necessary in the creation of compassionate 'speak up' cultures. Table 5.1 provides a template which can be used to: (i) guide critical reflection upon gossip narratives and episodes; and/or (ii) as a framework to develop further research questions – both of which can lead to the generation of practice-based knowledge.

Table 5.1 also has relevance as a training tool, for example, in support of the UK National Guardian's Office (NGO, n.d.), which leads, trains, and supports a network of 'freedom to speak up guardians' in England. The NGO was set up in the wake of a public inquiry into events at Mid Staffordshire NHS Foundation Trust (Francis, 2013). The public inquiry found that staff had tried to speak up formally about concerns, but had been ignored or victimized as a result, and that this experience was not confined to Mid Staffordshire. Freedom to speak up guardians provide an alternative route to speaking to a line manager/supervisor for all workers; expectations of the role are outlined in Figure 5.1.

A key component of Figure 5.1 is the need for freedom to speak up guardians to have *ring-fenced time* to effectively fulfil their role. The nine role expectations also give some pointers to areas for future research into gossip and the creation of compassionate speak-up cultures. For example, implications for leadership communication, barriers, and enablers of ethical speaking up, and the characteristics and contours of *'just gossip'*. Practice

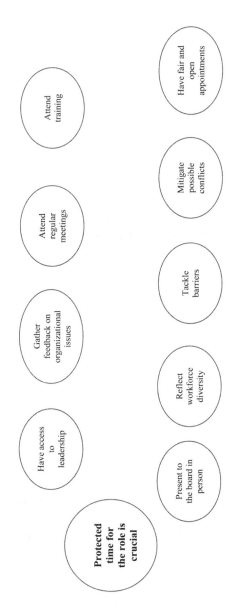

Figure 5.1 Expectations of the freedom to speak up guardian role. Source: *UK National Guardian's Office Annual Report 2018* (www .nationalguardian.org.uk; reproduced with permission).

Point 5.2 sets out some concluding assumptions for future academic-practitioner research.

Practice Point 5.2

Assumptions for future academic-practitioner research

- A workplace researcher is not the same as someone working in a laboratory.
- They are active participants in creating a particular story about how truth and power are spoken about.
- As we research with others, we may reimagine the way we – and others – understand the world(s) of organization and work.
- Research happens during everyday experience, not as a detached project.

Thinking and theorizing *triggered* by gossip can go in several plausible directions; researchers and practitioners will need to develop innovative ways of differentiating trivia from non-trivia, sense from non-sense, and meaning from the mundane.

Implications for future theorizing

Dewe and Cooper (2021) argue that the changing landscape of work and organization should act as a powerful reminder to researchers to ask 'not just where our theories are taking us, but how well they express the realities of working lives' (p. 66). Latham (2019, p. 15) also asks:

> Is there evidence that highly sophisticated theory has led to innovative or useful practice? Has the time come for the case to be made to our journal editors that studying context and practice will likely lead to useful inductively developed theories?

Arguably, research that comes from an academic-practitioner perspective will lead to useful, new, and practical theories and theorizing. There is also scope to bring fresh thinking to established cognate areas such as organizational discourse, narrative, and communication studies. I agree with Dewe and Cooper (2021, p. 83) who argue that our responsibilities now rest on 'beginning a process of challenging and refining accepted pathways'. To conclude then, when making new pathways in the emerging, and changing, landscape(s) of organizations and work in the COVID-19 era, there are three key questions to bear in mind:

1. What will be the purpose and utility of these new pathways?
2. Will the interdisciplinary terrain on which they are laid match that purpose, or does it need to be reorganized?
3. Where are the meeting points and intersections between practice and theory, science and art?

Final reflections

The aim of this book was not only to provide an overview of existing research and theory in the field of gossip, organization, and work, but additionally, to unsettle and disrupt traditional 'tried and tested' approaches. As a consequence, I have ventured outside my home discipline and comfort zones in work psychology and healthcare to explore other areas of researching, thinking, and theorizing. From a reflexive position, my values remain firmly in the field of practice, with a commitment to doing meaningful research to create useful knowledge that makes a difference in people's lives. I have had the opportunity to pause and reflect upon the importance of being courageous and candid about research and scholarship that matters. The outcome, I hope, has been to create an opportunity for ongoing interdisciplinary dialogue and debate about gossip, organization, and work, and the range of methods and methodologies that can be crafted, evaluated, and accepted in the business research community.

References

Adkins, K. (2017). *Gossip, epistemology, and power: Knowledge underground.* Cham: Palgrave Macmillan/Springer.

Alvesson, M., & Sköldberg, K. (2018). *Reflexive methodology: New vistas for qualitative research.* London: SAGE Publications.

Bain, R., & Mueller C. (2016). Understanding practice(s) and practising. In K. Orr, S. Nutley, S. Russell, R. Bain, B. Hacking, & C. Moran (Eds.), *Knowledge and practice in business and organisations* (pp. 30–42). New York: Routledge.

Bartunek, J. M., & McKenzie, J. (2018). Reviewing the state of academic-practitioner relationships. In J. M. Bartunek, & J. McKenzie (Eds.), *Academic-practitioner relationships: Developments, complexities and opportunities* (pp. 1–9). Abingdon: Routledge.

Bartunek, J. M., & Rynes, S. L. (2018). Narrative foundations for theorizing about academic-practitioner relationships. In J. M. Bartunek, & J. McKenzie (Eds.), *Academic-practitioner relationships: Developments, complexities and opportunities* (pp. 81–95). Abingdon: Routledge.

Beersma, B., & Van Kleef, G. A. (2012). Why people gossip: An empirical analysis of social motives, antecedents, and consequences. *Journal of Applied Psychology*, *42*(11), 2640–2670. doi: 10.1111/j.1559-1816.2012.00956.x

Beersma, B., Van Kleef, G. A., & Dijkstra, M. T. M. (2019). Antecedents and consequences of gossip in work groups. In F. Giardini, & R. Wittek (Eds.), *The Oxford handbook of gossip and reputation* (pp. 417–434). New York: Oxford University Press.

Ben-Hador, B. (2019). Social capital levels, gossip and employee performance in aviation and shipping companies in Israel. *International Journal of Manpower*, *40*(6), 1036–1055. doi: 10.1108/IJM-12-2017-0321

Boehm, C. (2019). Gossip and reputation in small-scale societies: A view from evolutionary anthropology. In F. Giardini & R. Wittek (Eds.), *The Oxford handbook of gossip and reputation* (pp. 253–274). Oxford: Oxford University Press.

Buick, F., Blackman, D., O'Flynn, J., O'Donnell, M., & West, D. (2016). Effective practitioner–scholar relationships: Lessons from a coproduction partnership. *Public Administration Review*, *76*(1), 35–47. doi: 10.1111/puar.12481

Burgelman, R. A., Floyd, S. W., Laamanen, T., Mantere, S., Vaara, E., & Whittington, R. (2018). Strategy processes and practices: Dialogues and intersections. *Strategic Management Journal*, *39*, 531–558. doi: 10.1002/smj.2741

Dewe, P., & Cooper, C. (2021). *Work and stress: A research overview*. Abingdon: Routledge.

Dixon-Woods, M. (2019). Improving quality and safety in healthcare. *Clinical Medicine*, *19*(1), 47–56.

Dunbar, R. (1996). *Grooming, gossip and the evolution of language*. London: Faber & Faber.

Edmondson, A. (1999). Psychological safety and learning behavior in work teams. *Administrative Science Quarterly*, *44*(2), 350–383. doi: 10.2307/2666999

Ellwardt, L. (2019). Gossip and reputation in social networks. In F. Giardini, & R. Wittek (Eds.), *The Oxford handbook of gossip and reputation* (pp. 435–457). New York: Oxford University Press.

Ellwardt, L., Steglich, C., & Wittek, R. (2012). The co-evolution of gossip and friendship in workplace social networks. *Social Networks*, *34*, 623–633. doi: 10.1016/j.socnet.2012.07.002

Eriksson, P., & Kovalainen, A. (Eds). (2016) *Qualitative methods in business research* (2nd ed.) London: SAGE Publications.

Farley, S. (2019). On the nature of gossip, reputation, and power inequality. In F. Giardini, & R. Wittek (Eds.), *The Oxford handbook of gossip and reputation* (pp. 343–358). New York: Oxford University Press.

Fox, M. (2011). Practice-based evidence – Overcoming insecure attachments. *Educational Psychology in Practice*, *27*(4), 325–335. doi: 10.1080/02667363.2011.615299

Francis, R. (2013). *Report of the mid staffordshire NHS foundation trust public inquiry*. Norwich: The Stationery Office.

Frost, P., Dutton, J.E., Maitlis, S., Lilius, J. M., Kanov, J. M., & Worline, M. (2006). Seeing organizations differently: Three lenses on compassion. In S. R. Clegg, C.

Hardy, T. B. Lawrence, & W. R. Nord (Eds.). *The SAGE handbook of organization studies* (2nd ed., pp. 843–866). Thousand Oaks, CA: SAGE Publications.

Gabriel, Y. (2015). Reflexivity and beyond – A plea for imagination in qualitative research methodology. *Qualitative Research in Organizations and Management, 10*(4), 332–336. doi: 10.1108/QROM-07-2015-1305

Gilbert, P. (2021). Creating a compassionate world: Addressing the conflicts between *sharing and caring* versus *controlling and holding* evolved strategies. *Frontiers in Psychology* [online]. Available at: 10.3389/fpsyg.2020.582090 [Accessed 1 July 2021].

Goetz, J. L., & Simon-Thomas, E. (2017). The landscape of compassion: Definitions and scientific approaches. In E. M., Seppälä, E. Simon-Thomas, A. L. Brown, M. C. Worline, C. D. Cameron, & J. Doty (Eds.), *The Oxford handbook of compassion science* (pp. 3–16). New York: Oxford University Press.

Green, S., & Andersen, H. (2019). Systems science and the art of interdisciplinary integration. *Systems Research and Behavioral Science, 36*, 727–743. doi: 10.1002/sres.2633

Harlos, K., & Knoll, M. (2021). Employee silence and workplace bullying. In P. D'Cruz, E. Norohana, B. Baillien, B. Catley, K. Harlos, A. Høgh, & E. G. Mikkelsen (Eds.), *Pathways of job-related negative behaviour* (pp. 201–229). Singapore: Springer.

Haroun, J. (2021). Flourishing in the university understory: Could compassion help? In K. Waddington (Ed.), *Towards the compassionate university: From golden thread to global impact* (pp. 102–118). Abingdon: Routledge.

Haskins. G., & Thomas, M., & Johri, L. (2018). *Kindness and leadership*. Abingdon: Routledge.

Hughes, H. (2019). Freedom to speak up – The role of freedom to speak up guardians and the National Guardian's Office in England. *Future Healthcare Journal, 6*(3), 186–189. doi: 10.7861/fhj.2019-0031

Jameson, J. (2019). Moving beyond 'homo economicus' into spaces for kindness in higher education: The critical corridor talk of informal higher education leadership. In P. Gibbs, J. Jameson, & A. Elwick (Eds.), *Values of the university in a time of uncertainty* (pp. 279–296). Cham: Springer.

Jex, S. M., & Britt, T. W. (2014). *Organizational psychology: A scientist-practitioner approach* (3rd ed.) Hoboken, NJ: John Wiley & Sons.

Kniffin, K. M., & Wilson, D. S. (2010). Evolutionary perspectives on workplace gossip: Why and how gossip can serve groups. *Group & Organization Management, 35*(2), 150–176. doi: 10.1177/1059601109360390

Kvernbekk, T., & Jarning, H. (2019). Mapping: Coming to grips with educational landscapes. *European Educational Research Journal, 18*(5) 559–575. doi: 10.1177/1474904119840181

Latham, G. P. (2019). Perspectives of a practitioner-scientist on organizational psychology/organizational behavior. *Annual Review of Organizational Psychology and Organizational Behavior, 6*, 1–16. doi: 10.1146/annurev-orgpsych-012218-015323

Leavy, P. (2020). *Method meets art: Arts-based research practice*. New York: The Guildford Press.

Lin, N., Cook, K., & Burt, R. S. (Eds.). (2017). *Social capital: Theory and research*. Abingdon: Routledge.

Marcus, B., Taylor, O. A., Hastings, S. E., Sturm, A., & Weigelt, O. (2016). The structure of counterproductive work behavior: A review, a structural meta-analysis, and a primary study. *Journal of Management, 42*(1), 203–233. doi: 10.1177/0149206313503019

McChesney, K., & Aldridge, J. (2019). Weaving an interpretivist stance throughout mixed methods research. *International Journal of Research & Method in Education, 42*(3), 225–238. doi: 10.1080/1743727X.2019.1590811

Microsoft (2021). *Work trend index* [online]. Available at: https://www.microsoft.com/en-us/worklab/work-trend-index/hybrid-work [Accessed 4 April 2021].

Morrison, E.W. (2014). Employee voice and silence. *Annual Review of Organizational Psychology and Organizational Behavior, 1*(1), 173–197. doi: 10.1146/annurev-orgpsych-031413-091328

National Guardian's Office (n.d.). *Welcome to the national guardian's office: Making speaking up business as usual* [online]. Available at: https://nationalguardian.org.uk/ [Accessed 4 April 2021].

National Guardian's Office (2018). *Annual report 2018* [online]. Available at: https://www.cqc.org.uk/sites/default/files/CCS119_CCS0718215408-001_NGO%20Annual%20Report%202018_WEB_Accessible-2.pdf [Accessed 4 April 2021].

Newman, A., Donohue, R., & Eva, N (2017). Psychological safety: A systematic review of the literature. *Human Resource Management Review, 27*(3), 521–535. doi: 10.1016/j.hrmr.2017.01.001

Nicholson, N. (2010). The design of work – an evolutionary perspective. *Journal of Organizational Behavior, 31*(2), 422–431. doi: 10.1002/job.603

Nutley, S., Bain, R., Hacking, B., Moran, C., Orr, K., & Russell, S. (2016), Concluding reflections: Exploring and mapping the knowledge and practice terrain. In K. Orr, S. Nutley, S. Russell, R. Bain, B. Hacking, & C. Moran (Eds.), *Knowledge and practice in business and organisations* (pp. 234–245). New York: Routledge.

Pheko, M. M. (2018). Rumors and gossip as tools of social undermining and social dominance in workplace bullying and mobbing practices: A closer look at perceived perpetrator motives. *Journal of Human Behavior in the Social Environment, 28*(4), 449–465. doi: 10.1080/10911359.2017.1421111

Poorkavoos, M. (2016). *Compassionate leadership: What is it and why do organisations need more of it?* Horsham: Roffey Park.

Poorkavoos, M. (2017). *Towards more compassionate workplaces*. Horsham: Roffey Park.

Reitz, M., & Higgins, J. (2019). *Speak up*. Harlow: Pearson.

Saad, G. (Ed.) (2011). *Evolutionary psychology in the business sciences*. Heidelberg: Springer.

Saad, G. (2020). The marketing of evolutionary psychology. *Journal of Business Research, 120*, 485–491. doi: 10.1016/j.busres.2019.03.048

Searle, R. H., & Rice, C. (2020). Making an impact in healthcare contexts: Insights from a mixed-methods study of professional misconduct. *European Journal of Work and Organizational Psychology* [online, ahead of print]. Available at: 10.1080/1359432X.2020.1850520 [Accessed 4 April 2021].

Seppälä, E. M., Simon-Thomas, E., Brown, A. L., Worline, M. C., Cameron, C. D., & Doty J. (Eds.). *The Oxford handbook of compassion science*. New York: Oxford University Press.

Serou, N., Sahota, L. M., Husband, A. K., Forrest, S. P., Slight, R. D., & Slight, S. P. (2021). Learning from safety incidents in high-reliability organizations: A systematic review of learning tools that could be adapted and used in healthcare. *International Journal for Quality in Health Care, 33*(1), 1–9. doi: 10.1093/intqhc/mzab046

Shea, S., & Lionis, C. (2017). The call for compassion in healthcare. In E. M., Seppälä, E. Simon-Thomas, A. L. Brown, M. C. Worline, C. D. Cameron, & J. Doty (Eds.), *The Oxford handbook of compassion science* (pp. 457–474). New York: Oxford University Press.

Simón, C., & Ferreiro, E. (2017). Workforce analytics: A case study of scholar-practitioner collaboration. *Human Resource Management, 57*, 781–793. doi: 10.1002/hrm.21853

Swendiman, R. A., Edmondson, A. C., & Mahmoud, N. N. (2019). Burnout in surgery viewed through the lens of psychological safety. *Annals of Surgery, 269*(2), 234–235.

van Iterson, A., Waddington, K., & Michelson, G. (2011). Breaking the silence: The role of gossip in organizational culture. In N.M. Ashkanasay, C. P. M. Wilderom, & M. F. Petersen (Eds.), *Handbook of organizational culture and climate* (2nd ed.) (pp. 375–392). Thousand Oaks, CA: SAGE Publications.

Waddington, K. (Ed.) (2021). *Towards the compassionate university: From golden thread to global impact*. Abingdon: Routledge.

Waddington, K. (2012). *Gossip and organization*. Abingdon: Routledge.

Waddington, K., & Kaplan, Y. (2021). Action learning as a vehicle for compassion. In K. Waddington, (Ed.), *Towards the compassionate university: From golden thread to global impact* (57–74). Abingdon: Routledge.

Waddington, K., Nowlan, J., & Kaplan, Y. (in press). Action learning as a practice: A case study of compassion in action. *EAWOP in Practice*.

Weick, K. E. (1989). Theory construction as disciplined imagination, *Academy of Management Review, 14*(4), 516–531. doi: 10.5465/amr.1989.4308376

West, M. A. (2021). *Compassionate leadership: Sustaining wisdom, humanity and presence in health and social care*. UK: The Swirling Leaf Press.

Worline, M. C., & Dutton, J. E. (2017). *Awakening compassion at work: The quiet power that elevates people and organizations*. Oakland, CA: Berrett-Koehler.

Index

Page numbers in **bold** denote tables, in *italic* denote figures

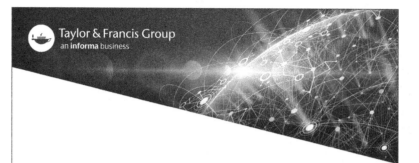

Taylor & Francis Group
an **informa** business

Taylor & Francis eBooks

www.taylorfrancis.com

A single destination for eBooks from Taylor & Francis
with increased functionality and an improved user
experience to meet the needs of our customers.

90,000+ eBooks of award-winning academic content in
Humanities, Social Science, Science, Technology, Engineering,
and Medical written by a global network of editors and authors.

TAYLOR & FRANCIS EBOOKS OFFERS:

A streamlined
experience for
our library
customers

A single point
of discovery
for all of our
eBook content

Improved
search and
discovery of
content at both
book and
chapter level

REQUEST A FREE TRIAL
support@taylorfrancis.com

 Routledge
Taylor & Francis Group

 CRC Press
Taylor & Francis Group

Printed in the United States
by Baker & Taylor Publisher Services